The

Sacred

Privilege

*Discover your ability, freedom, and power
to choose the life you want.*

MARK HEEREMA

THE SACRED PRIVILEGE

Published by Real Life Publishing
562-789-1909
Whittier, California

Copyright © 2007 Real Life Publishing
Library of Congress Control Number: 2007941584
ISBN 978-1-60530-438-0

Cover Design by Annsoorian

Editing, Composition, and Typography by Patti McKenna
Pcmckenna6@aol.com

This book is available at quantity discounts for bulk purchase.
For more information contact:

Special Note: "The Sacred Privilege" is designed to provide information and motivation to our readers. It is sold with the understanding, that the publisher is not engaged to render any type of psychological, legal, or any other kind of professional advice. The content is the sole expression and opinion of its author, and not that necessarily of the publisher. No warranties or guarantees are expressed or implied by the publisher's choice to include any of the content in this volume. Neither the publisher nor the author shall be liable for any physical, psychological, emotional, financial, or commercial damages, including but not limited to special, incidental, consequential or other damages. Our view and rights are the same: You are responsible for your own choices, actions, and results.

Printed in the United States of America

FOREWORD

Don Boyer

As an author, speaker and a publisher, I'm constantly required to make decisions. But, it's not those decisions which created my success. My success is the direct result of a choice I made a long time ago, when I was tired of living a life of struggle and chose to follow my passion. Like Mark Heerema, my passion is to help people to live fuller, more successful lives. Through my words, deeds, advice, and books, I've been able to do that. What was amazing, though, is that once I made the choice to dedicate myself to my passion, the success came. As a result, I live a fuller life, rich with family, friends, and business associates who also influence me.

Making the right choices isn't always easy, though. Some of the choices we make are habits; we choose to sleep on the right side of the bed or we always order pepperoni on our pizza. Others, however, can be mind boggling. Should I quit my job and start my own business? Should I apply for graduate school? Should I buy a new car and commit to five years of payments? Or, how about one of the biggest and long-term choices we make, should we have children? If so, when and how many?

In this book, Mark Heerema explains why we make the choices we do and then shows us how our lives are a direct result of those choices. For every action, there is a reaction; and for every choice, there is a direct result which impacts not only our lives, but also our attitudes.

Mark's message first came to me when he co-authored a chapter in one of our Power of Mentorship books, The Power of Mentorship for the Business Entrepreneur. Reading his contribution, I realized that we spend so little time weighing our choices; we don't even think about many of them. Then, we spend years dwelling on the results of those choices.

We can be the victim of our choices, or we can be the victor because of our choices. In this book, Mark uses relevant and enlightening examples of situations where a choice, good or bad, large or small, has affected lives of people like you and me. Some are victims, others are victors. But, they all have one common thread...they were faced with a choice that people have every day, and the path they took had a positive or negative effect based on that choice.

From morning to night, we're constantly creating our reality. The great thing about that is that we can recreate it any time and any place just by making better choices. Through this book, Mark Heerema gives us the knowledge to consciously make choices that will positively impact our tomorrows.

Like Mark and me, you, too, can be a victor because of your choices.

Don Boyer
Founder of the Power of Mentorship Book series
and creator of The Power of Mentorship, The Movie

The Sacred Privilege

At any time, anyone can change any part of his or her life as long as a person is willing to pay the price for it. For there has never been a person, regardless of physical condition, financial status, or education, in whom there is not possibilities for growth. It does not matter how many times one has failed or succeeded. Whatever is holding him or her back from their achievements can be overcome through personal choice. That opportunity each of us has, to choose our own path, is truly a sacred privilege, one we must not neglect, postpone, or misuse.

I am living proof that the power in personal choice does change lives. It changed mine, and it can change yours.

ACKNOWLEDGEMENTS

To my Lord and Savior *Jesus Christ*, who without his grace, mercy, love, and hope, I would not be here today. The light I see is only made possible through his amazing grace.

Amy, I feel mightily strong with you at my side. Marrying you was definitely the best choice I ever made. Thank you for your unending, selfless support as I pursue my dreams.

Mom, Dad, Kristin, and Reid, you are what family is all about. We have been through it all together and continue to build enormously strong love for each other. We are truly lucky to have our family!

Don Boyer, one day, I will repay you by giving to others what you are giving to me, that is invaluable, precious gifts of mentorship, guidance, and friendship. This book would not have happened without you.

Richard Fenton, this project really started with you and the encouragement you gave me to "just start writing!" GO FOR NO is truly inspiring, and you will continue to help many people through your teaching.

The Sacred Privilege
Table of Contents

INTRODUCTION

THE CHOICE THAT SAVED MY LIFE

I had it all. I was in my late twenties, happily married, working my way up in a thriving company, taking beautiful vacations, and thinking life was just too good to be true. I was living the "American Dream." Such was life, until one day my wife sat me down.

"I haven't been completely honest with you," she said. I didn't know what to say, and I remained silent as my mind tried to repress the possible scenarios of what might come next. Like any marriage, we had our normal ups and downs, but my belief was our problems weren't something we couldn't work through. "I have been having an affair," she said. Instantaneously, I found myself in an unimaginable reality. In my worst nightmare, I never anticipated my ears hearing those words. Betrayal as traumatic as that puts you in an unfathomable place—a place so deep and dark it is impossible to imagine.

Living alone in the home where our life together began, where our dreams were born, quickly became a lonely, dark cave filled with depression, anger, denial, and shame, all of which demanded my unwavering attention. Uncontrollable crying, severe mood swings, and being unable to stop thinking about my wife being with somebody else consumed my entire day.

All of my energy was directed toward figuring out what happened, how she could have done this, and why she did it. I had always been in control of my life, directing, guiding, and succeeding. Now, I was experiencing days so wretchedly painful I couldn't even muster up the strength to get out of bed. I felt powerless. I felt completely out of control. The polarity between the life I had enjoyed and my current state was shocking, to say the least. There was no end to my pain. Soon, life had little meaning. In such a short period of time, my life went from "How can this get any better," to "I don't know if I will make it through a day."

I just couldn't accept my new life. I still couldn't even contemplate this happening to me. Residing in the land of "tragedy" was completely foreign, and I had to come face to face with my new reality, a shattered heart and life. In a blink of an eye, I landed in a barren valley, not knowing where to turn or how to walk through it. There was no way out, no light, only pure darkness.

A few weeks later, my friend and I were walking along the beach. After shedding some tears, angry contemplation, and false justifications, I had created many stories, validations, and reasons to explain why this happened. He heard the whole story. The more terrible I could make her look, the better I felt. Finally, my friend looked at me after hearing my perfectly concocted story and asked, "Mark, what is God trying to do in you through this?" I stopped walking. I had never felt anything like it in my life. The piercing of those words into my heart felt tangible. Never before had words had such a physical affect on my body. The question seeped into my body like water into a sponge. I immediately knew something was about to change.

That night, I realized who I had become. I had chosen to be a victim of my circumstance. I turned into a blamer, a criticizer, someone who was great at finding reasons why I should look at everyone but myself. Up until that point, there were no reasons for me to look at myself. What did I do? I didn't do anything to deserve this.

That one simple question containing only eleven words changed my life forever. Everything came down to choice, my choice. I could look at my life as a victim, or I could take my situation and make the best of it. I knew at the time that adopting that outlook would be of benefit to me somehow someday. But, there was absolutely no way I could have anticipated the amazing power and lasting impact that one choice had.

Once I dedicated myself to the realization that I could choose my life, nothing has been the same. What was once the most difficult thing I ever went through or could ever imagine going through, has become the best gift I ever received. I never could have imagined becoming the person I am today, and I wouldn't be who I am had I not gone through the calamitous experience. My life is light years ahead of what I ever thought possible. I am married to an incredible woman, pursuing my professional dreams, and living each day as an adventure exploring for more. The bottom line? I had to first choose to accept the gift before it was mine. My new life today, full of joy, fulfillment, and hope, was only made possible by making a choice—the choice that my life will be whatever I choose it to be.

Why I Wrote This Book

I have always lived with a burning desire to help others maximize their life. I didn't realize it at the time, but ironically, the traumatizing experience I encountered was providing me with the precious gift I had always been searching for: a compelling, true experience that would allow me to help others.

One simple point that changed my life can change yours: personal choice. Once I began to see and experience the power choice had in my life, I felt a compelling passion and responsibility to share it with you. No one is exempt from making choices. It is an unavoidable part of life. Like most of us, I never fully grasped how powerful my choices were.

Choices do make and change our lives. That is why I find it amazing, exciting, hopeful, and inspiring that each of us holds in our hearts the treasure to achieve our hopes and dreams.

As life continues to afford us the freedom to choose our own path, we must take full advantage of the possibilities in every opportunity available to us. Truly, the ability we have to choose our life is a sacred privilege.

Self-help books and motivational seminars have helped me in many ways. I noticed that, in the majority of these books or seminars, experts make specific mention of how important choices are. Even before my research for this book began, I would read a paragraph where the importance of choice was discussed and then ask myself, "Well, how do I make better choices?" It was clear to me choices were important, but I didn't know how to apply that to my life in order to enjoy the results from good decision making. I assumed that with choice being mentioned as much as it was, choice was clearly an aspect of our lives that held significant value.

If I was thinking this, I was sure others were, as well. I dug deeper and found limited information on personal choice. I felt the invaluable lessons I had learned personally and professionally, plus a lack of resources detailing the everyday applicability of choices presented an opportunity to share a powerful message that is life changing. I am confident that the information you are about to read will empower you to live a more enriched life, a life you deserve.

What You Will Get From This Book

If everyone who reads this book was able to make just one improvement or learn one lesson that improves their life, I would consider this book a success. The lessons and information will provide opportunities to grow, and each of you will take away various lessons based on your needs or desires.

Synergy occurs when *something used together is greater than the sum of the individual parts.* A fitting example is our fist. If you had to punch through a wall, would you spread your fingers out or put your hand together and make a fist? Of course, the fist! It is much more powerful. Spreading your fingers apart and poking them at the wall uses the same amount of fingers; it just isn't as effective. The five fingers used together are much more powerful than each finger by itself. That is precisely how this book works. It is meant to be a synergistic tool. Not one chapter in this book will by itself equip you to effectively answer the question, "How do I make better choices?" The chapters have been designed in a specific sequence to lead you through a series of concepts and ideas that will provide you with a larger working knowledge of choices. Each chapter essentially serves as a step or way to make better choices.

To answer the question, "How do I make better choices?" is to really understand the importance and interdependency within each concept. Then cumulatively, when you have read and understand all of the concepts in their entirety, you will feel fully equipped to successfully improve your power of choice and understand how you can make better choices.

The concepts we will explore utilize a blend of personal and professional experience along with psychological reasoning. This balance works as an effective recipe to communicate the main ideas.

"That is what learning is. You suddenly understand something you've understood all your life, but in a new way."
Doris Lessing

Be Committed

You have a choice as to how you go through this book. What you get out of it will be directly in line with what you put into it. Are you going to be committed or just involved? There's an old riddle describing bacon and eggs that illustrates the difference between involvement and commitment. For the chicken, it only had to be involved.

Once it laid the egg, it could go on with its life and run the pen. But in order to get the bacon, the pig had to be totally committed. It had to sacrifice its life!

You could lay an egg and move on, or you could be totally committed to learning and achieving for your future. I know the resemblance isn't glamorous, but the more you can be like the pig, the more positive changes you will see!

There is an "Anti-Inertia Challenge" concluding each chapter. We know the chicken would look at them and move on. Don't be a chicken! Take the time to invest in your future. The action items were specifically designed to help you absorb the material and lessons you are learning.

Before You Go Any Further

Keep these five points in mind as you read the book:

1. The suggestions and information in this book are focused on how you can better make choices *over which you have control.* We all experience unavoidable scenarios we would rather have not encountered. Nicolas Watkins articulately stated:

"Take time to accept responsibility. Your life is exactly that – it's your life. It is created by you. You are constantly making choices, constantly creating new experiences. And although we can be affected by circumstances which can seem to be completely out of our control, essentially, we decide the direction in which we walk."

2. The word SUCCESS is defined by you! Anytime the word success is used, refer to your own definition of it.

3. As humans we operate from four areas of existence: spiritual, physical, social, and emotional/cognitive. In this book, you will be examining yourself from the emotional/cognitive dimensions. There will be areas that minimally cross over into the other areas, but the majority of material will focus on your choices through the context of the emotional/cognitive dimensions.

4. The teaching in this book will consist of topics that are "occurrences most of the time." Please do not read a section and claim it as false or dismiss it because it isn't "always" or "never" that way, and it wasn't prefaced with "typically" or "usually" or "for the most part."

5. We are all better when we are taught how to do something versus receiving a temporary boost of motivation. Change that is sustainable over a long period of time only occurs through learning. As exciting as a euphoric injection of motivation is, it is as quick as it is great. My hope is that you become inspired to improve your life as you understand how we create it, along with discovering the power within you to get it. The information is geared toward presenting you with lessons you can use for the rest of your life, ensuring long-term enjoyment and fulfillment.

We Are All Works In Progress!

One of the most valuable lessons I learned from a mentor was we are all works in progress. I don't care how "successful" we are, EVERY human being has areas where improvements could be made. The question isn't, "Do I have holes?" But rather, "Where are the holes?" Understanding that we are not perfect and accepting ourselves unconditionally serves one extraordinarily well, and giving ourselves that grace allows a healthier pursuit of self improvement. It was much easier for me to identify my weaknesses when I didn't beat myself up over them. Only then did I feel the complete freedom to abandon my insecurities and openly address my weaknesses.

As you complete the exercises in this book, areas of weakness will be exposed. Keep in mind, though, that is what makes us better. We can't patch a hole until we know where the leak is, right? Strive to improve a little bit everyday. Your life is not going to change immediately overnight. Habits you have had for years are not going to magically disappear. Make continual small investments in yourself everyday, and the cumulative results will be enormous. No one is better than anyone else. We are all works in progress and deserving of the right to make ourselves better everyday.

Everything is

or

involves a choice.

CHANGE YOUR CHOICES
CHANGE YOUR LIFE

> **Understand the power in choice. Realize you can harness that power to create your life.**

Our lives are predictable results of a cycle we unknowingly exercise constantly.

There is a "why" behind every choice we make.

Truly understanding ourselves is an essential aspect of choice making.

Choices are governed by universal laws. We need to be aware how they work and grasp their impact.

Specific behaviors differentiate people who live in fulfillment versus those who don't.

We all deal with adversity. How we choose to deal with it is the critical factor.

Choosing to exercise courage, discipline, a positive attitude, and persistence are vital to our choice making foundation.

Choice making becomes clear after we identify our desired outcome and detail specific steps to get there.

Chapter One

CHOICE:
THE FORGOTTEN FACTOR

*"One's philosophy is not best expressed in words;
it is expressed in the choices one makes. In the long run,
we shape lives and we shape ourselves. The process never
ends until we die. And, the choices we make
are ultimately our own responsibility."*
Eleanor Roosevelt

True stories are in italics. All the information and conversations are actual events. Only names have been modified to keep anonymity.

Breathing, Thinking, Choosing

Have you ever taken a moment to think about how many choices you make in one day? Have you ever contemplated the number of choices you had in one hour? More importantly, have you reflected on how those choices have impacted your past? How they impacted your present? How will they shape your future?

If you stop and think about how many decisions you make, coupled with their tremendous impact, it is truly astonishing. We are choosing all the time, and while we are choosing we are creating because:

**Every choice creates a result,
those results create our lives.**

It appears though, that we keep living among a huge discrepancy with choice. We make thousands of choices everyday, and those choices shape our lives, yet we do not take any time to truly understand them or ourselves in how we make them. Decisions occur so often, and we make them so fast that in an effort to keep up with life, we run forward without regard to what we are creating. Besides breathing and thinking, can you think of anything that comes close to the staggering number of choices we make?

Everything is a choice or has a choice involved in it. EVERYTHING! The famous existentialist Albert Camus jokingly remarked:

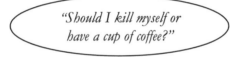

"Should I kill myself or have a cup of coffee?"

Some might think that comment is over the top, but Camus' point was simply that everything comes down to a choice. Some choices we are aware of, while others go unnoticed. Experts in the field of nueropsychology today agree that almost 95% of our daily behaviors are done unconsciously. Those are the decisions we make on "autopilot." The most basic and obvious example of a choice we make without much thought is choosing to put clothes on before we leave the house. Other choices though, such as what airline to fly or what we should eat for lunch, take more cognitive, deliberate thought. But, whether we realize it or not, we are making choices all the time, and all of our behaviors are a result of choices we make.

Let's take a small glimpse into how many choices we make during only the first few minutes we are awake. The alarm goes off and the game begins. If you're like me, the first choice you have is how many times can I hit snooze? Should I get up and exercise? What should I do first: shower, eat, or feed the dog? How hot do I want my shower water? Do I want breakfast? Do I want to eat it now or later? What do I want for breakfast? Should I shampoo or condition my hair first? Gel or no gel? What shirt will I look best in today? What pants? What belt? What shoes?

Can we conservatively agree that every minute we are awake we make 10 choices? I think it is much higher, but let's start low. If you want to plug in a number you think is more realistic, calculate away. We will use 16 hours per day, under the assumption that most of us sleep on average, 8 hours per night. Numbers, please:

Hours awake each day	16
Minutes in 16 hours	960
Choices per day	9,600
Choices per week	67,200
Choices per month	268,800
Choices in a year	3,225,600

Just think of the possibilities, based on this example alone, if you were able to make better choices only 5% of the time. You would definitely experience dramatic change!

It Boils Down to This

You can filter most, if not all of your choices down to this: we can either choose TO or choose NOT TO. Take reading this book. You either choose to read it or you choose not to. You will choose to do the action steps or you won't. On a bigger scale, you have to choose what you are going to do with your life! You want more? That requires discipline and sacrifice in which case you will be choosing TO do certain things and NOT TO do others. But, you can also choose NOT TO give yourself the success you desire.

Looking at a successful life versus an unsuccessful life from a black and white perspective, one would see that it takes just as much energy to devote oneself to being miserable, anxious, and down as it does to be optimistic, purposeful, and success driven. You do have a choice in all you do. You can either choose TO or choose NOT TO.

During our day to day life, it becomes to easy to feel overwhelmed by the hassles of the day: taking the kids to school, sporting events, paying the bills, seeing the dentist, selling the house, and all of the other thousands of life "fillers." Ironically, it is the "fillers" in life that distract us from choosing TO take the life we want. I have decided that in my life I am a TO person, not a NOT TO person. At the end of my life, I am going to look back and say I chose TO in life. What are you going to say to yourself? When you reflect back on your life, are you a TO person or a NOT TO?

Any Day I Want

A beauty that sometimes goes unnoticed in choice is that any day we want we can begin to make different choices. Choices make our past, present, and future so,

---

Whenever we want, we can choose differently.
That means anytime we want,
we can choose whatever we want!

There is nothing holding anyone back in this world from making a new start at anytime! Choices do not discriminate in their opportunity. The same possibilities are available to everybody all the time. We just need to decide when we want to start choosing differently.

Think about it, any day we want we can become whatever we want to be. At ANY time, we could decide TO read versus watch TV. We could decide TO exercise 10 minutes instead of sleeping. We could decide TO believe instead of doubt. Or, we could do absolutely nothing. We can choose to never change at all.

Everyday that we postpone making the successful decisions for our life, the longer we are going to have to wait for the results we want. If we don't like where we are in any area of our life – we can CHOOSE TO CHANGE IT!

Within You IS the Capacity for Success!

Kurt was a very talented individual to whom I would jokingly comment, "If I had your ability, I would be the President of the United States!" Like most of us, Kurt had very difficult challenges to overcome in order to achieve the life he desired. Abuse, divorce, and drugs were some of the obstacles he had in his storied past, making the road that much more difficult. But despite those adversities, he had so much talent, so much to offer to himself, his family, and to others. I marveled at his drive, energy, and passion. Kurt truly had so much potential; if only he could stay on course, he could change and claim the success he wanted.

One day after meeting with him, I began to reflect on Kurt versus another person who had a similar personality but opposite past. As Kurt continued to sludge through his life, I began to look for reasons why he couldn't pull out of it. The best justification I could come up with was his past, but that didn't sit well with me, despite my compassion for his pain. It was my way of letting him off the hook. Then it hit me: regardless how difficult the road, EVERYONE has the capacity to have a successful life. We always have the choice to choose TO or NOT TO.

**Greatness does not choose its suitors,
Rather its suitors choose greatness.
In this world that ability is within all of our reach.**

Yes, each of us has a different road with completely different obstacles and scenery, but we all have a road.

Kurt was intimidated by both ends of life. From the front, he was facing a fear of success, and from behind he was strapped by a terrible belief system limiting his future. I explained an analogy to him, which helped him understand that although the road was difficult, he had the power and tools to push through if he wanted.

Imagine we are all stuck in a ditch. The ditch represents our upbringing, every experience, all of our "stuff." For some, their ditch is only two feet deep, and to dig themselves out of their "hole" will take effort, but not blood, sweat, and tears. Others have ditches that we could term a well. The hole is hundreds of feet deep, and it seems impossible to ever make it to the top.

For every hole there is a ladder. Every hole offers us a way up and out. The ladder will be different lengths depending on the person. The point is we all have a way out of our holes regardless of how deep they are.

Like Throwing a Rock in the Pond

On a perfectly still morning, you are standing beside a pond so still it resembles a piece of unblemished glass. You drop a rock in the water. Ripples expand outward from the center in all directions. Eventually the ripples fade, but not until the area of water hit has increased tenfold out from the original drop. The ripple effect could be small or large, depending on the size of the rock.

Our choices are the rock. Every choice we make has a place in our life that is hit the hardest, the epicenter. But the results of our decisions do not stop there. They do not just affect that one part of our life. The consequences (positive or negative) move out from the epicenter, and into all other areas of our life, just like the rippled water. Choices we make do not only affect the obvious area. More areas of our life feel the results of the choices we make, regardless of how simple they seem.

The Obituaries

Try this exercise. You have the opportunity to write your own obituary. Take a few moments and reflect on what you would write if you were to die tomorrow. I know this isn't a rosy exercise, but it proves a point.

Take a guess as to what most people say is their greatest regret in life. Most commonly, people wish they had taken more chances, more risks. When I think of that, it makes me believe they shortchanged themselves by not pursuing their passion. How would they take more risks if they were given a second chance? By making different choices. They wish they had made different choices, which would have put them down different roads.

How do you want your obituary to read? Are you making the choices that will lead to an obituary you are proud of? Or, are your choices leaving you with an ending that is full of regret, emptiness, and unfulfilled potential?

Risk! Risk anything!
Care no more for the opinions of others, for
those voices. Do the hardest thing on earth
for you. Act for yourself. Face the truth.
Katherine Mansfield

Life Is So Unfair....Is It?

At times, life can seem so unfair. We look at the cards we were dealt and we feel like folding without the thought of placing a bet. Unforeseen circumstances, horrific situations happening to the best people, and life just beating us up at times takes its toll. However, can it be purely a coincidence that the people enjoying success just get lucky and avoid all difficulties? Do you think that life is more unfair to you? For a very select few yes, but for the majority of us, probably not. Truth: everyone faces trials, adversity, and times where life is just plain difficult. Life shares its unfairness with us all. Because we all experience it does not make it easy, of course. Did I think life was fair while my former spouse was with another man? Did I think it was fair when I was served with divorce papers? Of course not! I thought life was definitely unfair. But I soon found there were many people going through similar situations. Actually, the more I searched, the more I saw that many people had it worse than me.

Yes, life is unfair at times. We are dealt a hand that we didn't ask for. We are uncontrollably brought into occurrences we would want to avoid at all costs. Life equals out the playing the field, though, in that we all experience it's unfairness at some point in some way, and the only justification we have to make it fair is our ability to choose. No matter how unfair life is, regardless how difficult things become, we still, whether we like it or not, are fully responsible for our choices because:

Every behavior is a direct product of the choices you make despite how difficult things are.

Our lives are consequences of choices we make. Think about the "injustices" life has dealt you. How many of them are actually a result of choices you made? If you go to the root of the problems you are having, how many were caused by your choice?

Choices are such a vital piece of our lives. Choices can create us, break us, or build us; yet, we continue to ignore their power. Take ownership of your choices, of the choices you CAN and do make. The beauty is there isn't more you can do than that. There is great satisfaction in knowing you have done everything you could do. So remember, life is not unfair. In fact:

Life is fair because we all have the power to choose.

Those who have success in this life are not lucky. Life deals its unfair cards to us all, and you are no different.

"There are two big forces at work, external and internal. We have very little control over external forces such as tornados, earthquakes, floods, and pain. What really matters is internal force. How do I respond to those disasters? Over that I have complete control."
Leo Buscaglia

Anti-Inertia Challenge

Inertia: the inability to act.

Define your definition of success:

Without pretense, analysis, thought, possible or impossible, list all of the choices you would like to begin making today:

What is stopping you from making those choices?

Write out what your obituary would say today:

What do you want it to say?

What choices can you begin making to bridge the gap?

CHANGE YOUR CHOICES
CHANGE YOUR LIFE

Understand the power in choice. Realize you can harness
that power to create your life.

**Our lives are predictable results of a cycle we
unknowingly exercise constantly.**

There is a "why" behind every choice we make.

Truly understanding ourselves is an essential aspect
of choice making.

Choices are governed by universal laws. We need to be
aware how they work and grasp their impact.

Specific behaviors differentiate people who live in
fulfillment versus those who don't.

We all deal with adversity. How we choose to deal
with it is the critical factor.

Choosing to exercise courage, discipline, a positive attitude,
and persistence are vital to our choice making foundation.

Choice making becomes clear after we identify our desired
outcome and detail specific steps to get there.

Chapter Two

WHY YOU ARE WHERE YOU ARE

Doing the same thing over and over will
produce the exact same results again and again.

Studies now reveal that only 5% of our daily behavior is done cognitively. So, since we know that most of our lives are the result of habits, and we understand that when we have a habit we do it without thinking, and every behavior is a direct result of a choice, we can confidently conclude that we make thousands of choices without realizing it.

Where you find yourself today is not a coincidence, a fluke, or an injustice of life. Your current reality is a result of choices you made, habitual or not. Even though many of those choices are made without us being aware we are making them, there IS a reason you end up making that decision.

"You will never change your life until you change something you do daily."
Mike Murdock

There is too much at stake for us to live without comprehending how we make choices! Your current life is a mirrored reflection of all the choices you have made. When our current reality presents us with a reality we do not like (that could be financially, at work, in a relationship, spiritually, physically, etc.), you can begin to change that reality by looking at your "Reality Wheel."

This chapter is divided into three sections. The first part will explain our Reality Wheel. The second and third part will take two of the most important parts of the wheel, beliefs and habits, and examine them in more detail. What distinguishes beliefs and habits above the others is that beliefs serve as our foundation and begin the cycle, while habits are the end result and make up the majority of our current reality. There is more emphasis given to beliefs and habits, but do not underestimate the power of the other factors, they all are powerful influences on our life.

Part I: Explanation of How Your Wheel Operates
Part II: Examination of Your Beliefs
Part III: Examination of Your Habits

Part I: The Reality Wheel Concept

A phenomenal process occurs within our minds thousands of times a day. Every action we take is the end result of an intricate process our minds race through instantly. All of our action is inspired by a feeling. Our feelings are invoked by our thoughts, and our thoughts are inspired through our beliefs.

Beliefs ▶ Thoughts ▶ Feelings ▶ Action

So, where do habits and our current reality fit in? Well, we have already deduced that our habits are a result of our actions. We can then logically conclude that our current reality, or life, is a consequence of our habits.

Now our process looks like this:

Beliefs ▶ Thoughts ▶ Feelings ▶ Action ▶ Habits ▶ Reality

Why does the term Reality Wheel come into play? For two reasons, the first being based around the cyndrical shape of a wheel, and the second reason is based on the structure of a wheel. First, a wheel is circular in shape, which implies "ongoing." The final stop in the circle is our current reality, but the process doesn't stop there. Our current reality plays a significant role in shaping our beliefs, which connects the end of the process with the beginning, making it never ending once it starts, hence the wheel concept. If our current reality is depressing, that will likely reinforce or create negative beliefs about ourself. Conversely, if our reality is what we want, positive beliefs will be reinforced as the cycles continue.

A second reason the term Reality Wheel was created is due to the structure of a wheel. The spokes of a wheel return to a center hub while they also connect to the outer wheel. The center hub serves as our ability to choose, the command center, and from it, all of the spokes come in and go out. So interdependency is created between two points: where the spoke connects to the wheel and where the spoke connects to the hub. At each point then, a choice must be made before we move on to the next step in our process.

Here is an illustration which provides you with a visual of your reality wheel in its entirety.

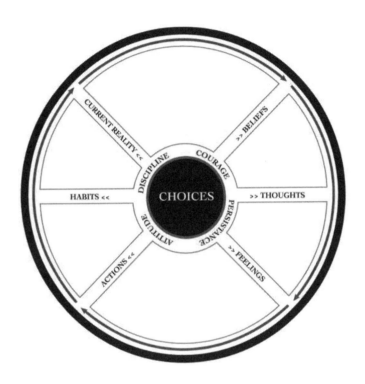

You probably noticed four behavioral traits revolving around the inner hub of choices: Courage, Discipline, Attitude, and Persistence. Going forward, these will be referred to as "life's irrefutables." In order to create a successful wheel, choosing to utilize these traits is absolutely essential. "Life's irrefutables" will be discussed in further detail in Chapter 8.

I'll walk through an example:

Belief: I am successful and worthy of all good things.
> *Choice: believe it or don't believe it.*
> *Choose to believe.*

Thought: I need to do things today to put myself in a position to succeed.
> *Choice: believe it or don't believe it.*
> *Choose to think it.*

Feeling generated: excitement, optimism, hope, inspired.
> *Choice: act on it or don't act on it.*
> *Choose to act on it.*

Action taken: search for opportunities, work hard, execute.
> *Choice: generate behaviors into habits or don't.*
> *Choose to build into positive habits.*

- **This process over and over again would create a habit.**
- **Habits then create your reality.**
- **Your current reality reinforces or creates beliefs, and the cycle continues.**

At every spoke in the wheel we have to choose what we will do. We are choosing our reality at every station. We speed through this process so quickly we aren't even aware it exists. But when we break it down at a micro level we get an idea how intricate and important the process is. Our choices move the process in the direction we move it, and the process creates our life!

Here's some good and important news. *We are only stuck in the reality we are in as long as we choose to be there. You operate your own wheel. You are in charge of creating your reality.* Whether your reality is incredible or flat-out depressing, we only remain in a reality because we choose to do so. Our lives are clearly and simply a mirrored reflection of our wheel.

Once started, the wheel, like our lives, doesn't stop or break. Unfortunately we are not granted any "life time-outs." There's no stop to the wheel once it is in motion. Life feels this way because just like our beliefs have an impact on our end reality, our end reality also creates and reinforces beliefs. Not only do your beliefs help shape your current situation, but your current situation also confirms and deepens your beliefs.

If you decide to change your beliefs then, does that change your current reality? NO! You have to choose at each stage in accordance with the belief to put yourself into the reality you want. But, the belief in which you choose to operate with has the most influence on the rest of your cycle. Your thoughts, attitudes, actions, and habits likely will follow in line with your beliefs.

It is easy for us to continue in the same pattern without recognizing it, and our patterns only deepen the longer we allow them to exist.

Imagine you are on a bicycle at the top of a steep hill. As soon as your friend lets go, you will begin accelerating down the hill. It is clear that once you start, you will slowly gather speed until eventually you are flying so fast you can't even see the spokes. That is exactly how we live in this process. When we are at the top of the hill and just beginning to move, we are too young to understand what patterns are being established in our minds by those we learn from. By the time we stop and say, "Hey, I want something different," the wheel is spinning around so fast it's hard to stop its momentum.

This analogy made more sense when I thought about real-life scenarios with people I know. Stop and think for a moment of someone you know who you believe lives a successful life (remember, you define success). Do they have a negative reality in some parts of their lives and an incredible reality in others? Probably not. Think about a person you know who you think has a hard time with life. Do they struggle because their current reality is bad? No! Their struggles are a result of how they process through their wheel.

Difficulties are a result of a negative process somewhere in the wheel, most likely beliefs. Positive actions will not be generated if beliefs, thoughts, and feelings are negative.

The reason for those consistencies we see in others is simple. Once your wheel starts moving, it gains momentum and the information we feed it, consistent with previous messages, only makes it move faster and faster until we do not even know our own habits that make up our life. That is why people who live rich lives consistently operate their wheel making the right choices, while those who struggle go through their wheel making the wrong choices. Whatever one's reality is, it receives continual reinforcement only until they choose to stop their cycle.

Experiment Time

For the next couple weeks, pick out people who you view as successful. Watch them and see if you can pick up on how their wheel operates. If you really want to dig in ask them some questions. The more you find out, the better your study. Also, find people who you think have a reality that is operating negatively, or one you do not want. Watch them, record your information.

Remember, our current reality is made up mostly of habits. Start with their habits and move backwards toward their beliefs. Follow their patterns. I have done this and the results are hardly staggering or surprising. Simply put, the people who I have monitored live a life in direct proportion to the wheel they have assembled. Show me your wheel, and I bet I can tell you your life!

Ouch...That Hurt!

I was riding on the handle bars while my friend roared down our favorite hill. We were flying. He kept peddling; we went faster. My feet were dangling dangerously close to the spokes, which looked like a blur of silver. One of my feet accidentally turned too far in and wham! The bike came to an immediate halt, sending my friend and me in the air. We came away very lucky with only a broken collarbone, a very sore foot that had the imprint of a spoke and a ton of scratches to show for it.

Your wheel is moving very fast now. Stopping your wheel will cause you some pain. There might be an accident or two. But, how else are you going to stop a fast moving wheel (sorry, no brakes on this bike)? If you want to change your direction you will need to put your foot in the spoke to stop the momentum. Anticipate that when you change a habit you WILL, not maybe, feel pain.

Part II: Beliefs

Our beliefs are THE MOST important part of our wheel because that is where the cycle begins. If a cycle begins in a negative state, your chances of executing a positive reality is extremely small, if not impossible. Beliefs unlock the treasure to an effective wheel, so modifying them where they are hindering our progress is absolutely vital.

Like all the material in this book, there is too much riding on the line, so diluting any message in an effort to sound "warm" would really be a disservice to you. That being said, as important as beliefs are, they are equally difficult to change. The difficulty in changing our beliefs comes from us reinforcing them thousands of times a day. Exercising anything that consistently and repeatedly definitely creates strong habits—probably the strongest habits we have. Time, energy, patience, and persistence will be needed in order to change beliefs; however, the results you will experience in your life by changing your beliefs are worth every ounce of energy and time.

We Own Our Beliefs

A great story that illustrates the point of beliefs is this example by life coach, Drew Rozell.

One evening, a Native American chief was speaking to his tribe; and he spoke of two dogs that existed within his mind.

One was a white dog, good and courageous. The other, a black dog, was vengeful and full of spite. The chief told the group that the two dogs were engaged in a constant battle. When asked by a brave, "Which one of them will win?" the chief responded, "The one I feed."

This simple story makes a valuable point. That is, I am going to believe whatever I choose to believe. In other words, *you have control over your mind!* Yes, every part of the body has its unique functions, but your mind is just like your foot, arm, or finger in that it is all a part of a bigger sum. The wisdom of the Chief was that he realized he was not his mind. His mind didn't control him, rather he controlled it, and it was up to him to feed it the food HE wanted. You are not your mind. You don't have to believe your current beliefs! They can be changed.

"If you believe you can....you probably can. If you believe you won't...you assuredly won't."
Dennis Waitley

We are each products of our own beliefs. What you choose to believe will shape your thoughts, actions, habits, and life. Whichever set of beliefs you decide to feed will be the one that grows because your beliefs will be justified in what you do. You will look for reasons to support your beliefs.

If you don't believe, you don't achieve.
If you believe, you will achieve.

I Believe

"You have to expect things from yourself before you can do them."
Michael Jordan

Beliefs are the beginning of our wheel. In order to begin changing the choices we make, we must first deal with the root of our problems. Our current life is ultimately the result of our beliefs. If we started first by jumping immediately to our habits, we would be dealing with only the symptom and our change would likely be unsustainable. It's the same as if we go to the doctor because of a broken arm. The doctor could prescribe us a pain killer, which would alleviate the pain. But our pain is only the symptom from the broken arm. True healing will only take place if the root problem is addressed, setting the broken bone. If you decide to create positive habits but your beliefs are negative, that contradiction will abort your desired process. Alignment of your wheel is imperative to its working effectively. Each process must be on the same page in order to move forward.

In order for our wheels to work:

1. **The spokes must be properly aligned with one another. That starts with beliefs.**

2. **The root has to be addressed: your beliefs.**

(Given that every person's beliefs are different based on so many variables, some belief systems can be handled through

41

individual persistence, while others might take professional help. I am a very strong advocate of professional counseling. Through my darkest days, I was fortunate to invest in a weekly session that allowed me to make progress I could not have made on my own. If you do decide to seek out professional help, remember to first interview candidates. Not every therapist is right for you. It's your choice! Second, remember that a good counselor will not tell you the answers, they will lead you to your own).

If a Five-Year-Old Can....

Martin was a self proclaimed grouch. One day while working outside with his five-year-old daughter he screamed at her for wildly running around. Her response was quite interesting. She told her daddy that she used to be a whiner, but when she turned five, she decided that she was not going to whine anymore. Her final punch to her father's gut was, "and daddy if I can stop whining, you can stop being a grouch."

This simple insight by a five-year-old not only transformed Martin's life, but it triggered a whole new field of psychology, a field Martin Seligman would coin, "positive psychology." Dr. Martin Seligman has become a world re-known psychologist, today known as the father of positive psychology. (Dr. Seligman has written many great books. One I would suggest on this topic would be, "Learned Optimism.")

Old Beliefs vs. New Wants

There are many times in our lives when we decide that we want more of something or different circumstances. An event occurs that triggers re-evaluation, and we see things from a new perspective. We declare to ourselves, "Out with the old and in with the new!" The problem is we commonly underestimate the power of our current beliefs. We aren't aware of how deep the roots have established their stronghold.

(All true stories are in italics. These stories are told to help emphasize a point and to illustrate how the concepts play out in real life. In no way, are any stories meant to demean or harm one's character. All names have been changed.)

Wendy, a young woman in her mid twenties, joined the sales profession. Like so many others, she had a storied past. But, Wendy seemed different. The drive and desire that I saw in her was more than the average person. Despite seeing many people fall victim at the feet of old beliefs, I believed she would win. What I saw surprised me. Wendy and I both underestimated the powerful undercurrent of a negative belief system. Despite intense desires for change, her beliefs held miraculous power over her behavior. Her poor belief system undermined any positive effort in seconds. Before undertaking this new career in sales, we spoke at great lengths discussing how difficult the journey would be, especially while carrying emotional baggage.

It seemed as soon as things were going in the right direction for Wendy, her exuberance and positive direction would be gobbled up by the demons in her mind. Sadly, Wendy was unable to get past her deep-rooted negative beliefs. She serves as a great example of how such wonderful people can be harmed by such negative processes.

Your old beliefs have deep roots. They have reinforcements behind them. Even though we want to get rid of them, in a sick way they are comfortable, you become used to living with them because that is where you are used to going.

Fighting the fight with your desire for the new or different is like being in a foreign country not knowing the native tongue. You have no roots with the new, only the desire of what it is you are looking to attain. Put your boxing gloves on; it's going to be a fight, but a fight you can win!

How Do We Change Beliefs?

There's good news and bad news. Bad news first: changing our beliefs is very hard work. Good news: all you have to do is change your "story." Our beliefs are *only* the story that we tell ourselves. We are the narrarator of our own story. That means we can write the script, right? YES! Negative beliefs are only negative stories we believe because we have told them so many times. The more we hear them, the more truth we give to them, and the more we ultimately live them out. What makes this even better is that the stories we tell ourselves aren't even true! So why not change the story you are telling yourself to whatever you want your story to be?

**We can listen to any story we want,
so, let's tell ourselves a great story!**

People make a living helping people change their beliefs, which might make them not too happy with me here, but this IS true. Get creative. In order to recondition your mind from years of telling the same stories it will take time, discipline, patience, and the telling of new stories. Listen to hypnotherapy CD's; talk into a microphone every night repeating beliefs you want. Write down a belief you want every morning. Start with one, but try it for thirty days. It will work! Also, try and catch all of the negative, false stories you tell yourself. They happen more than we realize. Write them down. Discount them and turn the story around to your favor.

Part III: Habits

Habit Formation

A habit is a learned behavior that becomes second nature after repetitive repetitions. Since a habit is something learned, it seems logical to examine the way we learn to understand how our habits are formed. There is a sequential series of steps that we typically evolve through to end up with a behavior being a habit. Here is the sequence:

Step 1: Unconsciously Incompetent or Ignorant
(We don't know that we don't know)

▼

Step 2: Consciously Incompetent or Aware
(We are aware that we don't know)

▼

Step 3: Unconsciously Incompetent or Practice
(We are unaware we know)

▼

Step 4: Consciously Competent or Habitual
(We are aware that we know)

▼

Step 5: Unconsciously Competent or "Autopilot"
(We do it without thinking about it)

Step 1: During the first step of learning you are not even aware you don't know. So, you don't know that you don't know. Think back to before you sent your first email. Before sending out your first virtual communication, you didn't know how to send the email and you didn't know why you didn't know. Then your friend comes along and introduces this cool new concept called email.

Step 2: You go to a computer and the friend shows you how to send an email. At this point you still have not sent an email but you have a basic understanding of the process, and now your fear begins to subside as you become more familiar with the process.

Step 3: Now that you know what to do, you start emailing your friends on your own. Even though it still feels a bit unfamiliar you are beginning to improve. Frustration can easily set in at this stage because your improvement isn't always easy to see. But more and more practice brings you to Step 4.

Step 4: Your learned behavior has now become a habit. I bet most of you today can send an email in about 3 seconds. Think back to how scary your first few were! You didn't know who would get it and how.

Step 5: At this point, you can perform sending an email so quickly you don't even know how many you send. We have reconditioned our mind! It becomes something that feels instinctual, action without cognitive thought.

Habits are learned, so they can be unlearned, too!

How Do You Know if You Have Good Habits?

How do we know if we have good habits? The most obvious answer would be what you have accomplished in a particular area of your life. Sometimes though, it is hard for us to be objective with ourselves. In an attempt to protect ourselves we manipulate and massage false truths and formulate deceptive lies regarding our own performance.

Here are three questions that I challenge you to direct toward all important aspects of your life. Complete honesty is crucial. We'll use "money" as an example. Please interchange "money" with any thing you wish.

Question #1: What results have I accomplished with *money*?

Question #2: Am I satisfied with my results?

Question #3: If you answered "yes" to #2, start again with a different part of life. If you answered "no," then you must decide: do you want to do anything about it? What are you going to do?

Try this out just once. You will see results after you scale it down at this level.

Habits Create Your Reality

I think it is safe to say that most people would like to make more money. Who making $55,000 per year would not want to make $100,000 a year or more? Who making $125,000 a year wouldn't want to make $200,000 a year?

Do you know the percentage of Americans that annually make over $100,000? Around 5%. That's right only 5%! That means that only 5 out of every 100 people accomplish that. Do you know how many people make over $250,000 a year? Less than 1%.

Let's pretend we are going to do a study on those 5 people who make more than 100K in annual salary. What do you suppose their Reality Wheel looks like? I would bet the main difference between people not making six figures and those that do is simply habits. The people who earn six figures or more a year have learned and dedicated themselves to a consistent, productive cycle that produces consistently positive results.

The more I experience life, the more stingy life seems to become at giving what I want or expect. There is no such thing as easy anymore, is there? In fact, life is so stingy that I have found the greater the reward or desired result, the more I need to give to acquire it. Let's not fool ourselves here, the people whose reality we admire have developed good, strong habits. Those habits create their reality and future. Anything they enjoy in abundance is simply one of the collateral benefits of their habits. Why does their life look so easy? Why does success always seem to "find them?" For the same reason that professional actors make acting look easy, or how easy professional golfers make hitting a golf ball look easy. They have mastered what they do, and their consistency produces amazing results that make their actions look easy.

We will become whatever our habits are. Negative habits will lead to negative consequences, just like positive habits lead to positive consequences.

Your current reality should not be a surprise to you when you honestly assess your habits.

Our realities are a predictable outcome of our habits. If you were to tell me your habits, I will tell you your reality. The quote in the beginning of the chapter says it best. You are insane to even imagine things being different if you are not willing to change the way you do things. That is insanity! Your reality will only change if you change the way you exercise it!

Cross Functionality of Habits

We all reveal our habits in many obvious ways. For instance, I can gather some solid probabilities with how organized a sales professional is by seeing some very small details. Little things like the inside of their car, personal hygiene, their dress, or their carrying case tell me most of what I need to know. Consistent most of the time, this is an example that habits are cross functional. In other words, how you do something in one area of your life is how you will do it in another.

I have yet to meet someone who is immaculately organized at work and has a sloppy home. I have never seen it! If you are responsible at home, you probably have those skills as a professional, as well. Your habits carry over. Your habits are not designated to individual segments of your life.

How we do anything is how we do everything.

Building New Habits

So, we understand habits are a critical piece to creating the reality we want. How do we do that? Just like you, I have a hard time breaking old habits and inducting the new habits I want. These suggestions have helped me achieve what I want.

With new habits, we need to:

♦ Rededicate ourselves every day to our goal.

♦ Understand your habits experience. The longer you have had a habit, the longer and harder it will be to break.

♦ Ask for help! Accountability goes a long way.

♦ Start small, build confidence and successes first!

♦ Always break big things down into smaller, digestible pieces.

In breaking old habits, we need to:

♦ Know what situations, thoughts, etc. trigger your habit and stay away!

♦ Change your situation to avoid being vulnerable.

♦ Try and find different responses to your emotional habits.

Talk Is Cheap and Intentions Are Weak

Scott was adamant about changing his current reality. He clearly understood the cycle and was aware of the challenge ahead. The good news for Scott was he had become so desperate and sick of his family being in such despair he finally decided enough was enough. It was exciting to anticipate what Scott and his family could experience should he make the necessary changes. We didn't know what would happen, but he had the first step ready: the motivation to have new.

The first few days following Scott's revelation produced serious behavioral and attitude changes, and by no coincidence sales results followed. But shortly a problem arose. It wasn't a catastrophe by any means. Just a problem one would expect to incur who was living in this type of reality. Unfortunately, the problem was big enough to swipe Scott off his feet. Despite his initial resolve for change, any problem was simply too much too overcome. He fell back into his old reality.

Approximately a week later Scott excitedly informed me he was ready to go back at it. "Great!" I exclaimed still believing and hoping this time it would happen. Again, a few days of discipline, hard work, and good choices culminated in successful selling. But as life would have it, another monkey wrench came flying in. Scott knew he had a choice, but he just couldn't withstand the pressure and he surrendered again. Scott could never overcome the inevitable "curve ball." Some of the challenges were brought about by the reality he had created, while others happen to anyone. The cycle can be vicious, unrelenting, and addicting; but it is very possible to get out. Unfortunately, Scott could not.

Intentions are only ideas.
Until they are acted upon, they are nothing.

This example is not meant to undermine Scott's effort or desires. I applaud his heart and empathize in his struggle.

Like Scott, I have many times excitedly committed to a new motivation only to be suddenly halted in my own tracks. It is terribly sad to see someone who does have good intentions to change not be able to follow through. We can see it, taste it, smell it, and imagine it, but we have a very hard time GETTING it. I can't even begin to count how many things I had the *intent* of changing, only to surrender under pressure, like Scott.

Intent without follow through will leave us in one place: where we started.

We all share this common sequence of behaviors with intention and adversity:

We start with a new intention. That develops into:
▼
New behaviors. Inevitably, we run into:
▼
Challenges. And we oftentimes:
▼
Revert to our old form. We then get:
▼
Frustrated again with our situation.

The initial trigger for a new behavior is usually a crisis, new information, or a realization. But even with determined motivation, small problems easily detour us. Ultimately, after cycling through this numerous times, we give up on our intended behavior. The hardest part is pushing through the adversity and to not give in to what seems easiest and that is to revert to our old habits.

**Do not expect to get better or
attain new without having to fight
through unforeseen challenges.**

Remember, intentions are really only ideas. What if Mr. Franklin only intended to invent electricity? What if Mr. King only intended to be a civil rights activist? Get the point? Take action. Expect trouble along the way and fight through it. By themselves intentions are weak, but combined with action and resolve, they are the beginning of a new life.

Anti-Inertia Challenge

Identify the key areas of your life and think about your current reality. Is it where you want them to be?

What habits have you allowed yourself to acquire that are responsible for creating that reality?

Examine your beliefs. What beliefs are negatively affecting your reality?

What actions can you begin taking to change your habits?

List some difficulties that you might have to overcome as you change your habits.

What thoughts, feelings, and beliefs will you need to begin fostering in order to achieve your desired reality?

Identify intentions you are holding onto that have not experienced action.

CHANGE YOUR CHOICES
CHANGE YOUR LIFE

Understand the power in choice. Realize you can harness
that power to create your life.

Our lives are predictable results of a cycle we
unknowingly exercise constantly.

> **There is a "why" behind every
> choice we make.**

Truly understanding ourselves is an essential aspect
of choice making.

Choices are governed by universal laws. We need to be
aware how they work and grasp their impact.

Specific behaviors differentiate people who live in fulfillment
versus those who don't.

We all deal with adversity. How we choose to deal
with it is the critical factor.

Choosing to exercise courage, discipline, a positive attitude,
and persistence are vital to our choice making foundation.

Choice making becomes clear after we identify our desired
outcome and detail specific steps to get there.

Chapter Three

WHY WE MAKE THE CHOICES WE DO

There IS reasoning behind the choices make.

Digging into the "why" behind our choices requires us to take a psychological approach. There are logical and behavioral explanations for why we choose what we do, and in order to improve our choices, it is imperative to understand the reasoning behind them. Additionally, properly identifying our "why" is an essential precursor to change. Without understanding the root cause, we would fail to address where the real problem lies.

Think about it like this. You or someone dear to you comes down with a rare disease. Due to the rarity of the illness, no one knows what the disease is. What is one of the first things we do? Yes, we would jump on our computer and research it. We would find out what the sickness means, what it is, the cures, and everything else imaginable. We try and take the mystery out of it. We know the research itself and acquired knowledge will not change any conditions, but we still have a desire to demystify its meaning. Even the smallest bit of understanding dissolves the mystery and gives us a sense of control during a time where we feel we have none. So why then, given the amount of choices we make and the impact they have on our life, don't we understand why we make the choices we do? Because, undoubtedly, becoming privy to what is happening "behind the scenes" will shed new, undiscovered light we need to see.

Equipping ourselves with a more knowledgeable understanding of our psychological tendencies and behaviors will not make better choices for us by itself. Rather, *it will provide us with a better understanding of our behavior.* This awareness will present us with more opportunities to make new and better decisions.

Choices are made so quickly and so often that we rarely understand or notice the process that is behind them. But if we slow our thinking down and tune into our patterns, we will see ourselves in many of the ideas discussed in this chapter. Know that you are not alone here. Everybody falls into these patterns. That is why psychologists have terms and explanations for them. Let me also encourage you to open your "insides" up so new realizations may be realized which will lead you down new paths of success.

Pleasure vs. Pain: A Weighted Scale

Before I go to bed at night, I will have grandiose plans of what I am going to do the next morning. I'm going to wake up at 4:30 a.m. and save the world! Then, while sleeping like a rock, I hear the dreaded sound, the alarm. Really? Already? I quickly remember my plans for the morning, then I begin to think about how cozy my bed is. It is now that I get into trouble. I begin to weigh my options.

Hmm. Getting up out of bed and exercising sounds painful. It's about as likely as me dancing with the Jackson Five. But staying in bed, which sounds totally pleasurable, is about as likely as the sun rising. I soon find myself easily leaning toward staying in bed, or in other words, what sounds more "pleasurable" than "painful."

I absolutely dreaded doing the dishes before I had a dishwasher. There were times when I would rather make another trip to the store to buy plastic plates than to clean up the sink. It took monumental motivation to make me move on that. In fact, it was probably one of the things I procrastinated to the worst degree. But then, doing the dishes met its match. I walked into the kitchen one morning, and I saw something resembling a tower; it was a stack of dishes that almost hit the ceiling. I ventured over to my computer to start writing my first paper for graduate school. That too, seemed exceedingly painful. It was my first "homework" in years. I didn't realize how painful I perceived starting my paper until I thought, "I think I should do the dishes!" It was the first time ever when washing the dishes sound like a good idea! Why? Because writing that paper was more painful, there was fear. There was less pain in doing the dishes, and that's how I made my decision.

We gravitate toward what we feel will make us experience the most pleasure as we simultaneously move away from and try to avoid pain. Even when a decision involves only negative consequences, most often we look for the result that carries less pain. We are creatures who seek and find pleasure. We are always looking for ways to feel better. It is obvious then why we are vulnerable to choose in the direction of pleasure even when we know it is not the best choice.

The choices we make will usually answer the question, "What will make me feel the best?"

However, easier does not equate to better. Look at consumer debt in America. People without money spending money. Why? They think buying things will make them feel better.

It is simply a pursuit of pleasure. People look for ways to experience happiness even at the expense of feeling pain in the future. It is truly fascinating when we take a detailed look at just how much pain we will inflict on ourselves in the future in order to enjoy pleasure in the present.

Another principle that stands out in regard to how we negotiate our pleasure and pain is:

We take action when the pain of not changing exceeds the pain of changing.

You have a co-worker at work who is not pulling their weight, but their tenure with the company cuts them some slack. Basically, over the years, this employee has become lazy in their job, doing just enough to get by. Retirement is only a few short years away, and everyone knows this individual is simply counting down the days. It is also widely understood that the company will reciprocate the loyalty card by paving the easy road to the finish line. Sweetening the pot further for this employee is a generous pension plan with extravagant benefits. But suddenly new management comes in. The new boss gets a quick read on the situation and is more concerned with producing results than rewarding loyalty. They inform the employee that if their performance does not change, they will be forced to terminate them. What happens next is quite predictable. The employee's performance suddenly improves. Why? If they didn't change, they would lose their job, the benefits, and the pension plan they had planned their golden years around. At that point, the pain of being terminated clearly becomes more painful than changing behavior. This employee would perceive implementing new behavior less painful than looking for a new job and recouping the other losses. That is why their behavior would change.

The Devil Made Me Do It

In making choices, we justify our emotion with logic.

"Mark, I have to make more money" Beth stammered as she fought back tears. "I don't know if I can stay in sales. It's not paying the bills." I suggested we take a look at her expenses and finances in more detail. After some digging, we came across some recent extravagant purchases that most would call luxurious, which surprised me given her earlier statement about money. Beth told me she was taking her son on a trip as a reward for achieving good grades. I gently inquired about the necessity of that given her current financial state. "Mark, I had to," she responded. " I couldn't not do anything!"

We all know the feeling. A parent's deepest desire to take care of their children and give them everything they want. But Beth truly felt like she HAD to take this trip and justified it by saying and believing she had to. Beth didn't HAVE to do anything. She WANTED to! Telling herself "she couldn't not do it" was a justification to avoid feeling guilty. It was easier for Beth to justify it by claiming she had no choice versus facing the reality that maybe there was another way to reward her child. Like all of us, Beth's emotions defeated logic. We are creatures of emotion. That means we make decisions based on how we feel.

Our choices are not made from a position of logic.
They are made from a position of how we will feel.

First, we decide what we want, then we figure out a way to justify that decision with logic. You decide to start eating better. Your first trip to the store after your newfound zeal is exciting. The question isn't, "What fruits and vegetables will I get?" But, "How many fruits and veggies will fit in my cart?" While making your rounds, you mistakenly stumble across the cookie aisle. Oops. You stop when you make eye contact with your nemesis, Mr. Chocolate Chip Cookie. Without realizing it, you present a logical argument to yourself to fill your emotional desire. You rationalize to yourself, "Well, if I am going to eat good ALL the time, I need to have at least something good once in a while." Before you can say "cookie" the bag is in your cart. You just sold yourself into believing that you NEEDED those cookies! It was just a matter of providing yourself with some logic to make the decision.

Emotional want ▶leads to ▶ Logical justification

Protected Area: Keep Out

Closely related to our ability to validate emotion with logic is what the psychological world refers to as cognitive dissonance. Cognitive theorist Leon Festinger concluded that human beings have a need to feel a strong consistency between our thoughts, words, actions, and values. So when we do something that might compromise that consistency, we search for a valid reason that will negate any emotional discomfort. Essentially, we all look to protect our self and the values we hold.

For example, you take pride in the fact that you do not gossip. It is one of the values you hold true to your heart. In the break room, you come across some information about someone you despise. Your temptation rises as you feel the information is too good to keep to yourself. Your temptation wins out. Immediately after you tell your friend, shame and guilt cover you like a blanket. You quickly feel you "sold out." A slight nausea sets in. The discomfort you feel is a failure of alignment between your actions and your values. Then, to help make us feel better about our misalignment, we look for rationale behind what we did so we feel decent about ourselves. That rationale might sound something like, "She won't tell anyone anyway." Or, "Someone else would have told her eventually." This is cognitive dissonance at its finest.

Learned Helplessness

In the 1960's, the father of positive psychology, Dr. Martin Seligman and his collaborators performed a study that produced remarkable results. The experiments were focused on studying the basic learning processes in animals. The study consisted of three groups of dogs. Groups one and two received a shock and then could jump to the other side of the cage to avoid another shock. Group three however, was given a shock, and when the dog would jump to the other side, it would receive another shock, as well. Basically, the first two groups of dogs could avoid the shock while the third group, no matter where they were, would get shocked. A very short time later, the dogs had a chance to reveal what they learned. The experiment was run again. Not surprisingly, the dogs from the first two groups remembered to jump to the other side to avoid future shocks, but the third group of dogs, instead of jumping to avoid the pain decided to lay passively dormant until the researchers stopped the experiment! They didn't even make an attempt to escape their condition! What did Seligman and the other researchers conclude? When it came to controlling their fate, the animals had come to believe that the shocks were inescapable and nothing they did made a difference.

The conclusions from this study have had a profound impact on what we now know about helplessness. You can learn and believe that you do not have control. Additionally, and maybe more importantly, the animals *transferred this learned helplessness to a new situation, one where they did have control.* When this happens, the implications and missed opportunity could be enormous. Understand that:

We are rarely rendered helpless, and we have more control over our environment than we realize.

I Want It Now!

Do you know what economists believe to be the number one contributing factor to why people spend more than they have? *People's inability to delay gratification.* That is the same reason why we make many choices we know we shouldn't. We live in a society where everything is available at our fingertips. When asked to wait, we get impatient. We are all used to having everything better and quicker.

As the time that it takes us to get things becomes shorter and shorter, the ability to delay gratification becomes harder and harder.

For our ancestors, it was a different story. They didn't have a plan for their future. They could only be concerned with how their daily necessities were going to be met. Where will we get water? What animal will we be able to hunt for

64

dinner? But now that our lives can be put on credit cards, there isn't a worry about our basic needs being met. Naturally then, since most of us know our basic needs will be met, we look for the extra pleasures in life. At times you might feel that your long-term objectives are limiting you from getting your daily "feel good." You want to experience pleasure, and you want to feel good now!

A study was done at the University of Stanford where four-year-old children were placed in a room one-by-one. A marshmallow was placed in front of each child. The children were told if they were able to wait fifteen minutes to eat the marshmallow they would get a second one. Guess how many ate the marshmallow anyway? Two out of every three.

Fifteen years later, a follow-up study was conducted. The findings were incredible. The children who had the ability to refrain fifteen minutes from eating their marshmallow were having more success in life. Conversely, those who were not able to wait were more likely to have been a school drop-out, have poor grades, and incur far more debt.

The ability to discipline yourself to delay gratification now in order to enjoy greater rewards in the future is an absolute prerequisite for success.

Don't Bother Me. I'm In "The Zone."

If you are or have been involved in sports, you are probably familiar with the phrase, "in the zone." It refers to a time when everything goes perfectly. Everything one does or touches is seemingly perfect. At work, you come up with good idea after good idea, a salesperson having a magical quarter, a basketball player sinking continuous shots, or a baseball player hitting home run after home run are all examples of being "in the zone."

Unfortunately, the zone being referenced here is not a positive zone. It is the allure of comfort we fall into which inhibits us from growing. It is the choices we make because we're comfortable that stop us from becoming what we could. When we live in our "zone," it only limits our potential.

Did you know that our brain actually can actually become addicted to the status quo? Did you know that one of our brain's main functions is to protect us? Our own brain fights us to stay in our comfort zone. We don't have to be our brain! What your mind tells you is in no way the law. Feel free to tell yourself, "Thank you, but no, thank you!"

There are other contributors that make it easy for us to stay in our zone: pleasure and fear. Here's an analogous example. Todd is a very successful banker. In his life, he has achieved numerous awards; but outside of the office, Todd hopes to be more courageous. He has lived most of his life as a "city dweller" and has never been comfortable to venture into the outdoors. His friends challenge him to get out of his comfort zone of the city and try climbing a mountain nearby a cabin a friend owns. Todd is an ambitious fellow and doesn't like to back down. Plus, the sound of "stepping out" sounds exciting. He eagerly accepts the invitation. Todd makes the trip to the mountains during the winter and is nervously excited at his friends' challenge. The thought of climbing the unknown mountain does strike fear in him, but the anticipation of stretching himself and accomplishing something new is invigorating. Before the climb, Todd and his friends are enjoying a nice, warm fire in the cabin. They are talking finances, investing, and other matters involving work. Minutes before his climb, he straps on all his clothes, gear, and other necessities. Todd starts to feel trepidation. He steps his foot outside the warm cabin and is immediately taken aback by the cold, swirling, biting air. After a quarter mile hike in treacherous conditions, he decides it is best to head back to the cabin where it is warm. His hiking partner, an experienced mountain climber, assures Todd everything is fine. Their hike is clearly marked on an obvious trail. Despite his friend's confidence, he convinces himself the climb is not that important to him. Todd tells his friends he is disappointed that he wasn't able to make the climb, but secretly inside feels glad to be back where it is safe. What would Todd have seen if he pushed himself out of what felt comfortable? What could he have experienced?

Your comfort zone = no growth zone

We have all been like Todd. What is your "cabin?" What is the mountain you need to climb? The allure and pleasure of our comfort zone so easily seduces us, and fear so easily precludes us from doing what we need to do. Watch out for your comfort zones! Check yourself in the choices you are making to see if you are living in the warm cabin.

"I want to stay as close to the edge as I can without going over. Out on the edge you see all kinds of things you can't see from the center." Kurt Vonnegut, Jr.

Your Actions Speak So Loud
I Can't Hear What You Are Saying!

Observational learning is a term that says much of what we learn as humans is a result of what we observe in the world around us. Early in life, children are told by their parents, "Do as I say, not as I do." Unfortunately, children are sharper than they appear because they do learn more through modeled behavior than spoken words.

American psychologist Albert Bandura ran an experiment designed to test just how powerful modeling was for children. The experiment revealed that children who first watched adults beat up a large doll were far more aggressive in their play with the doll compared to children who had watched more gentle play or no adult at all. Also interesting to note is that the children didn't just imitate the physical beatings they saw, they actually devised other unique ways of torturing the doll. They saw the message that aggressive behavior was accepted and acted along those lines.

Professional psychologists posit that the behavior modeled to us was the most powerful during the years when we were the least aware. Sounds a bit unfair, doesn't it? That means today, when we are aware, we are making choices based on the modeling we experienced when we weren't aware. We can logically deduce then, that a significant portion of our behavior is due to conditioning we didn't know was occurring. We were too young to rationalize what we were seeing. Irregardless, what we saw as children, we learned, and what we learned, we now act upon as adults.

Utilities

You go see a movie with a friend. The two of you walk out, and what is the conversation? "Did you like it?" We decide if we enjoyed the experience or not. During the movie, how the movie made you feel is called experienced utility. But before leaving for the movie, you had to choose what you were going to do before you could do it. You had to select a movie based on what you expected the experience to be, or how you thought it would make you feel. This is called expected utility. Then, once you have had the experience, your future choices will be made from your remembered utility, what you remembered about the experience.

Daniel Kahneman, a Nobel-Prize winning psychologist, has proven that two things will determine what we remember about our pleasurable experiences. First, how we felt when the experience was at its "peak," and second, how we felt when the experience ended, or "peak-end." This peak-end is usually what we refer to later on to recall our feeling of the experience. It serves as our summary. These summaries then in turn serve as large influencers in future choices.

Here's an interesting study that further reveals this phenomenon. People were asked to listen to a pair of very loud, uncomfortable noises through headphones. The first noise lasted eight seconds and the second sixteen. The first eight seconds of both noises were exactly the same. But the second eight seconds of the second noise were not as loud. The participants were later told they would have to listen to one of the noises of their own choosing again. Which one do you think the majority of participants chose? If you are like me, I would say the first. Just get my eight seconds done with already! Remarkably, a higher number of respondents said they would rather hear the second noise versus the first. Why? The second had a more pleasant end and, consequently, the participants remembered it as less uncomfortable than the first, despite listening to disturbing noises for twice as long.

Feeling Blue? Can That Choice Wait?

There is scientific evidence confirming that our mood affects how well we make decisions. Feeling negative, for example, will narrow your focus, will make it more difficult to see all of the possibilities, and most likely limit your focus on a limited number of parts contained in a choice.

On the other side, recent studies have shown that a positive mood will elicit better decision making; the better your mood, the better your thought process. You will be more open to new possibilities and more likely to consider various alternatives.

Adaptation

"If I could just get into this place, everything will be so much better," Rob told me. A couple months later, I asked him, "So, are you still enjoying your place?" The answer was a less than desirable, "Yeah, it's all right." This is called adaptation.

I asked a frugal friend of mine why he was set on always leasing a car rather than buying. "Because I want a new car every two years," he answered. "I get tired of them around that time." After an undetermined amount of time, we get used to things. Basically, our desire and passion for them dwindle until we need something new.

Adaptation is why the shirt you bought a year ago and have worn 12 times does not elicit the joy you experienced when you first bought it. It's the reason why that car you are driving now, which was once the envy of the neighborhood, seems like a debt-buster rather than a nice car. Adaptation is the reason why you begin to feel dissatisfied emotions about your house that just four years ago was your "dream home."

The process of adaptation by itself is not the problem. Trouble occurs when we are unable to anticipate it and realize it is happening. For whatever reason, we seem surprised when we end up feeling displeasure toward something we once could not live without, even though this process happens to us over and over again.

Here's an easy way to remember it:

we want → we get → we get used to (adaptation) →
we want new

**Simply being aware of adaptation is a strong antidote.
Remember, it is natural and insatiable.**

Mispredicting Satisfaction

I knew I only had three classes left before the completion of my master's degree. The possibilities of what I would be able to do with the time I had spent studying for the last two years was exhilarating. I couldn't wait to enjoy the feeling of completion. I could sense just how sweet life would taste when I was done. It was as if I was being released from prison and would finally experience freedom. Finally, I finished. I waited for this magical feeling I had anticipated to come through me for so long. Good thing I wasn't holding my breath. The feeling never came. Life kept moving forward. It was obviously apparent to me then that I had poorly predicted how I was going to feel. I thought I would feel way better than I ever did.

College students in the Midwest were asked about what they thought it would be like to live in California. Their results showed that they believed students in California were happier than students in the Midwest. An amazing climate and more satisfaction in life were the main reasons they gave. The participants were right about the weather, but not about students from California being happier in general. Good weather does not disintegrate debt, rent, second jobs, tough exams, and romance problems.

A large number of the choices we make involve a prediction about a future emotional state. Similar to the students in the above case, it is easy for us to misinterpret satisfaction. When we do this, it can make for bad decisions, especially when the decisions revolve around big ticket items.

Your Quality World

World renowned psychologist William Glasser wrote a thought-provoking book titled "Choice Theory." I want to mention a piece of his idea here because it touches on why we make certain choices.

Glasser explains that although we see the world very similarly to others, it is not the same world. As we live, we create pictures of people we want to be with, things we want, and a set of beliefs or ideals. This unique world to us is what he calls our "quality world." It becomes the best way to satisfy our own personal needs. Since we want to feel the best we can, we do our best to assure that everything we choose puts us in our quality world.

For example, your child plays on an athletic team. For you and the other parents, you see the field the same because it is not part of anyone's quality world. The field is the field. But when it comes to your child's performance, your quality world's take over; and from there, you see completely different games and skill sets. Because they are part of your quality world, you will see your child's performance very differently than your neighbor. Whether other parents agree with your opinion of their performance is irrelevant, because you define your reality in how it works best for you.

Why is this important? Because many of our choices are based on having the world fit into that quality world. When decisions living in your quality world become the main criteria for making decisions, you can easily fall into trouble because your decision-making criteria is compromised by the false pretenses of modifying life to fit into the world you have created.

Mental Models

You ever catch yourself saying things like, "I don't trust people," or "celebrities are stuck up," or "I can't stand Monday's" (that's more like it, huh?)? Those are what Peter Senge refers to as Mental Models. Senge explains that mental models are not how we make sense of the world, but rather what determines us to take action. A mental model is a basic generalization or assumption we make which dictates our behavior. Don't believe me? Try this on for size. You have a mental model that people are untrustworthy. Can't we agree that a person who holds this model will act, treat, and communicate with others differently than someone who does trust people?

Whether our mental models are right or wrong is irrelevant. What's important is that we are aware of their existence.

Senge further digs into mental models by examining interpersonal ways we can exploit ourselves. We have what he calls leaps of abstractions. A leap of abstraction occurs when we take an observation to a generalization without validating it as truth. An assumption becomes a fact.

A co-worker was at a trade show and witnessed an owner of a competitor dealing aggressively with an employee. My co-worker quickly came over and explained what they had seen. Without being privy to any facts about what happened, we both jumped to the conclusion that this owner treats his employees poorly. I later realized that we had made this erroneous conclusion from only seeing one part of the story. It's very plausible that the employee made an error or didn't correctly service a customer's needs. The point is we didn't know the whole story, yet we jumped to a conclusion from limited evidence.

Feeding Your Self Image Tapeworm

Our set of beliefs, combined with our self worth, can lead us in a potentially dangerous direction of making choices that will fulfill predictions we make based on how we feel about ourselves. In the psychological world, this is known as a self-fulfilling prophecy. Isn't it amazing that we can actually cause something to happen by believing it will occur? This prediction, of course, does not become true by coincidence, but as a result of the choices made and actions taken in order to make true what we believe.

Say on your way to work, a fresh cup of coffee spills over in your car. After the four letter expletives explode out of your mouth, you begrudgingly admit to yourself, "Today is going to be one of those days." During the course of the remainder of that day, you look to find experiences and manipulate them to reinforce that belief.

Like adaptation and mental models, the danger with self-fulfilling prophecies is that they lie unnoticed in the corner of our minds. The beliefs we try to prove correct can be devastating. Dangerously, these prophecies we hold secretly work behind our conscious mind and direct our actions in many unrealized ways. Check yourself and see if you can detect any negative prophecies you have projected out and make sure your choices are geared toward completing positive self-fulfilling prophecies.

Anti-Inertia Challenge

List places in your life where it is evident your choices are made in order to avoid pain.

Where are you most susceptible to validate emotion with logic in order to get what you want?

Are there areas of your life where you have learned to be helpless?

When do you have the most difficulty delaying gratification?

What are your comfort zones? How can you get out?

What modeled behavior did you learn when you were young that you don't always realize you exhibit? Which behaviors do you want to change?

Do you hold any mental models you would like to get rid of? Are they backed with evidence versus assumptions?

Does your past indicate that you are feeding negative self-fulfilling prophecies? Where are those beliefs coming from?

CHANGE YOUR CHOICES
CHANGE YOUR LIFE

Understand the power in choice. Realize you can harness
that power to create your life.

Our lives are a predictable result of a cycle we
unknowingly exercise constantly.

There is a "why" behind every choice we make.

> **Truly understanding ourselves is an essential
> aspect of choice making.**

Choices are governed by universal laws. We need to be
aware how they work and grasp their impact.

Specific behaviors differentiate people who live in fulfillment
versus those who don't.

We all deal with adversity. How we choose to deal with it is
the critical factor.

Choosing to exercise courage, discipline, a positive attitude,
and persistence are vital to our choice making foundation.

Choice making becomes clear after we identify our desired
outcome and detail specific steps to get there.

Chapter Four

YOU, MEET YOU

***Most people choose to live their entire life without
understanding who they truly are.***

The bulk of our behavior is a consequence of habit. That
makes it difficult to accurately assess just how connected our
reality and habits are. I think if that connectedness was
more tangible, the impact of our habits would be much more
noticeable. Since it isn't so obvious, enhancing our self
awareness becomes a critical piece of our choice making
puzzle.

This section, "You, Meet You" is written for the purpose of
gaining a deeper understanding of yourself. Through this
understanding, I hope you will be able to uncover some
deep-seeded thoughts, behaviors, and habits which when
dealt with, will help you to begin to make positive changes.
After completing this chapter, you will have:

1. A deeper understanding of yourself, which will
   provide you with more accurate insight into why you
   make the choices you do.

2. More clarity into past patterns and what future
   possibilities might bring.

3. A more profound insight into your vulnerabilities, strengths, weaknesses, predispositions, and genetic make-up.

4. A clearer picture of what things you will be able to change (behavioral) and what you can't (genetic).

5. The ability to grasp the intimate interdependency between your actions and your reality.

Carrying False Assumptions

A large group of Chinese Ambassadors had come to America to address a high-ranking group of American Government officials. Before the address, there was a banquet dinner. In honor of the Chinese guests, a formal Chinese meal was served. At one of the corners of the large rectangular table they placed an American next to a Chinese man. Soup was the first course served. After finishing their respective bowls of soup, the American attempting to make any conversation looked at the Chinese Ambassador and asked, "Like Soupie?" The man looked at him and did not reply.

When the meal was over, it was time for the Chinese to address the Americans. The Chinese man from the corner stood up and walked to the platform. He then delivered a speech in absolutely perfect English to the American man's astonishment. Walking back to his place at the table, the Chinese Ambassador looked at the American and asked, "Like Speechie?"

If you don't closely examine your deeply-rooted assumptions, you will never see that many of them are distorted or flat-out wrong.

We all carry false assumptions. We "leap" to them without knowing. Our brains work so fast the process is unrecognizable. The assumptions we develop do not come out of nowhere. Our perception or series of perceptions, in other words how we see the world, shape our assumptions. From there, we have a choice. You can either validate your assumption based on facts or evidence, or you can validate your assumptions based on what you want to believe.

Are You a Walking Discrepancy?

Denise was plodding through her forties, supporting herself with a very mediocre salary. She had been in sales for almost eight years, but had not fully grasped the opportunity. The last few years, her sales numbers had remained flat. I believed that, with a few small tweaks she could easily achieve her desired success, but as in all cases, it was up to her and she knew that. At the beginning of a new year, Denise came storming into my office exclaiming, "I am going to make $100,000 this year!" "Great!" I responded.

We went on to outline a detailed and progressive plan that would put Denise on her way. Before she left I asked her, "Are you sure this is what you want?" "Yes, I am positive," she excitedly said. The reason for my asking is because she had worked in sales for eight years without much improvement or desire to improve. I was excited with her but skeptical, provided her track record.

The first few weeks she was well on her way; then she totally collapsed. Her balloon popped, she ran out of gas, and slowly her behavior returned to her previous levels. A couple weeks later, I had her into my office to discuss her recent performance. I explained to her that although I greatly appreciated her effort and that I wanted her to want more from herself, her behavior screamed that she didn't truly want more. For if she truly wanted more, her actions would follow.

There was a vicious battle between what she thought she wanted versus what she was willing to do.

In addition to the discrepancy of what one thinks they want versus what one truly wants, is the discrepancy between what one wants and *what they believe they can have*. I see many individuals with the best intentions in the world. They have plans to rule their worlds but lack the self-esteem or belief system to carry it through. If you are fighting that battle, you first need to work on your core beliefs. Nothing changes on the outside until the inside is clean.

Whatever is grown and nurtured on the inside will manifest itself on the outside.

If our discrepancy is between our self beliefs and what we want, it is imperative to first decide how bad we want the results. Once your beliefs are aligned with the outcome, the intended results will follow.

Ask yourself these questions to identify discrepancies. If you have them, think what you can do to resolve them:

1. What do you want?
2. Are you willing to do whatever it takes?
3. What action have you taken to validate that?
4. Are you able to do what it takes?
5. Why do you want it?

If you haven't taken any action yet, why not? What's holding you back? Some discrepancies occur because we convince ourselves we want things because society or others want them. Identifying the truth behind why you really want something is of prime importance. If your reasoning behind an effort is not sustained by a powerful "why," you will find yourself in a situation similar to Denise, a fight inside.

Polygraph Test, Please

I choose to carry myself as a very positive person, as I am convinced optimism is an invaluable tool for life. I also am a big advocate of honesty. It seems the two get easily jumbled in an effort to keep things harmonious. Honesty is compromised in order to keep things optimistic. But we need both. We need to be realistic with ourselves while, regardless of circumstance, remain optimistic about our future. Overall, we are not honest with ourselves. Sometimes, the lies we deceive ourselves into believing are so far off from the truth it is scary!

It's a terribly sad thing to see a single dad who is supporting children having to suffer through making a living, especially while earning their income in an emotional game like sales. Tom was divorced and in his early forties with two children. In the middle of what was turning out to be a difficult month, I called him. "Hey, Tom, how are things; what's going on?" I was surprised by his response. "Really good, how are you?" I appreciated the optimism, but I was more concerned with his future. "What do you mean, good?" I asked him.

He had some serious challenges to deal with and, yes, his optimism was great, but it was robbing Tom of looking at his situation honestly. By failing to be honest, he was not addressing weaknesses that were hindering his performance, which hurt himself and his family. At the expense of his and his children's well-being, Tom was taking every measure to protect himself by lying about his feelings and current state.

Optimism and reality. Remember we want our thoughts, actions, behaviors, and values to be in line with one another. His way of keeping himself in "alignment" was to pretend everything was okay. This was dangerous and didn't force him to take accountability for his situation. As long as he was deceiving himself, he would never have to look at why things weren't okay. His deception allowed him to stay in his comfort zone, even though it was a chaotic one. Admitting that there are problems is good because then one can say, "How do I fix this? But until then, nothing will change.

You will never fix what is wrong until you can be completely honest with yourself.

Ole Svenson conducted a telling survey. Eighty percent of the drivers surveyed rated themselves in the top 30% of all drivers. Huh? That means that 50% of respondents had an inaccurate view of their driving ability. We are all dishonest with ourselves in order to keep some sanity upstairs. Like Tom from the example above, when we are dishonest with ourselves in an effort to keep mentally aligned, we are only robbing ourselves of making improvements in needed areas.

"You cannot fix what you will not face."
James Baldwin

Acknowledge Truths

If a co-worker and yourself were given questions to rate you on your work ability, whose score do you think would be higher? You would score yourself higher, right? This is true because generally we hold a higher view of ourselves than how others view us. This reality we carry can lead us into believing false truths. Here's a good exercise for you that will provide a more accurate assessment than our own thoughts do (because past performance is the best evidence we have). Write down the major events in your life that have most contributed to where you are today. Are these indicative of what you want or are trying to accomplish? Aside from your thoughts, what story do your results tell? Is it different from what you think your results are? Look for patterns. They will reveal truth. Try and identify consistencies. Do you end up in certain situations regardless of where/how you start? Truly, we behave more consistently than we know, regardless of how great our thoughts tell us we are.

The most accurate assessment of the choices we have made are the results in our life, not what our thoughts tell us.

I was interviewing candidates for an open sales position for a new territory. John, a young man in his early thirties, enthusiastically applied for the job. Although John had never set the world on fire, I thought maybe a change of scenery would infuse him with a much-needed emotional boost. He had been with the company for a few years and was excitedly thinking about transferring to this new location. Through his experience in the industry, John had the type of "plug and play" material any company adores. So, it made sense that we speak about the opportunity. After the normal formalities, we discussed the transfer *to the new city, and then came the topic of money. The most money John had ever made at the company was $55,000, so I assumed he would expect something in that range as well. I asked him, "So, John, what are your thoughts on your salary?" "I will go sell in the new territory for $90,000," he confidently answered. "I would like that type of raise too," I thought to myself. After gathering my thoughts, I responded, "John, the most money you have ever made here is $55,000. I believe you can make $90,000 and much more if you applied yourself as we know you can. However, until you prove to me you are worth that, I am not going to pay you that money."*

Ambition wasn't John's problem. He wasn't willing to acknowledge an obvious truth. That is, up to that point, in this particular job he was producing sales resulting in his pay. He truly felt his production was worth $90,000, but, in reality, he had never exceeded $55,000. Was he capable of making $90,000? Of course, everybody is. The point is his performance was completely out of sync with the reality he created. His production and his perceived value were way off base. Those gaps are easy to create and believe the longer we choose to live in them. Be careful with yourself. What does your life say about your choices?

Consciousness

The term "consciousness" deals with how effectively we are able to be aware of what is happening around us, and more importantly, *within us*. Being aware of what is happening around us isn't too difficult. We do that naturally. But being fully aware and understanding what is going on inside of us is a completely different and more difficult idea.

Let's expand our definition of consciousness so it applies more directly with choices. Let's define it as:

"Developing the ability to understand our beliefs, thoughts, and behavior so we can freely choose, instead of choosing based on what we were programmed to be."

When was the last time you asked yourself these questions around certain behaviors (especially habits affecting your reality)? Below are three simple questions you should ask yourself as frequently as possible:

> Why do I do that?
> How could I do it better or differently?
> Why do I choose to do it that way?

For some of us, it's a conscious decision to avoid looking inside because what's inside is too much to deal with. There is tremendous pain for many of us, and some things seem better untouched. That doesn't exclude us from looking at other areas we could address and improve. Also, consider that whenever we decide to bury an unresolved issue that affects other areas of our lives. Further, understand that living with those issues will impress upon our behavior, therefore, deeply imprinting who we become and slowly compromising the person we were meant to be.

For others, we don't look because we are too lazy. You say you want better things in life, like more money and big houses, but aren't willing to exert the energy to start at home plate, with your own self.

"The unexamined life is not worth living."
Aristotle

Tapping into your consciousness gives us a newfound power and freedom. We have all heard the phrase, "knowledge is power." Well, this is a chance to give yourself power with yourself. By deepening our consciousness we will be able to better understand our thoughts and feelings. With that understanding, we are in a much more effective place to begin making choices which will produce positive change.

You Are Your Own Best Friend

I went to eat at Taco Bell. My favorite is a bean burrito with sour cream and no onions. I gave the cashier my order, paid, and stepped aside. While I was walking away, I heard the guy behind me begin his order. "I'll have a bean burrito with extra onions and no sour cream." I chuckled as I realized that was the exact opposite of what I ordered. How funny, I thought. For each, their own. Neither burrito was better than the other, it was just personal taste. The experience itself is insignificant to say the least, but the lesson was profound. We are all different, all unique, and we need to love ourselves just for who we are.

Many days, we are our own worst enemy. That's everyone else's job, isn't it? My job is to be my best friend. At certain times, it can feel like the entire world is against us, so why would we compound that by beating ourselves up as well? How do you treat yourself? Are you your best friend? Do you love yourself unconditionally just as you are, strengths and weaknesses alike?

Years ago, a timeless book was written titled, "I'm OK – You're OK," by Thomas Harris. The book is a detailed study on coming to grips with yourself and others. If you battle with self-esteem issues, I strongly suggest you invest in this book. Simply put, we encounter enough peanut galleries every day from others; we don't need another.

No one cares about you like you do.
Be your own best friend. Love yourself unconditionally.

Don't Give Away Your Power

I challenge you to chart how many times you hear people give away their power. Give away their power? What?

"I really had to…," "I just didn't have time," "I haven't been able to get around to that yet," are all phrases where we communicate we didn't have control of our time or behavior. The problem with that is we are communicating that lie to others, and worse, we are convincing ourselves of that truth. When we are unaware that we operate this way, it puts us in a powerless position. Remember:

We all have time to do things we want to do.
If we want to do something, we will do it.

Within reason, we all have the choice to do whatever it is we want with our time. "I couldn't get to it" just isn't true. What you really mean is, "I decided to do other things." Within all of us lies the control to do whatever we want. We don't have to do anything! I have time to do whatever I choose to do! I challenge you to chart how many times you hear others and yourself give away power. It's an easy slip that occurs too frequently. Of course, at times these phrases are made in jest. Someone asks you, "You want to go to lunch?" Our response isn't, "No, I don't want to" even though it might be true. We respond appropriately, "Thanks for the invite, but I am slammed today." We really might be extremely busy, but if we want to go to that lunch, we will!

Don't give away your power with messages that allow you to feel like you don't have control. Everyone has 24 hours in a day, and that time is filled up with choices and actions we feel are the best for us. Whatever those choices are is fine – just take responsibility for them and know you are in control.

Have You Had Your Eyes Checked Lately?

You and a friend visit an art museum. You come across a piece of art that grabs your attention. You turn to your friend to see if they see the same picture. "Isn't that amazing?" To your dismay their response is something like, "It's OK." Is the picture any different depending on who is looking at it? Yes and No. The picture obviously doesn't change. The difference in the picture is the perspective of the person looking at it.

We've all been involved in situations where the desired or anticipated outcome didn't happen. After a sales meeting, I will ask the other sales person their thoughts. Nine times out of ten, we will see a different situation and opportunity. Why? Because we all see the world through our own lenses shaped by our unique experiences.

We see the world as we are, not as it is.

Our glasses are tainted, dimmed, and tarnished by experiences, modeling, jobs, friends, and of course, beliefs.

That is why so little in this world is matter of fact and why so much is a matter of opinion.

Did you know there are still people today who think the world is flat? The group is called The Flat Earth Society. Despite overwhelming scientific and physical evidence confirming the opposite, they hold true to their belief that the world is flat. It doesn't matter what is, as long as they choose to hold the belief the world IS flat.

Everything and anything is what we believe it to be.

We know our beliefs can be changed, and we learned that many of our beliefs are shaped when we are too young to filter through them. So, we could look at negative beliefs as simply lies, illusions, or beliefs we have not had the opportunity to validate yet, right?

Earlier, we established that whichever beliefs we feed will grow, and that we do have a choice with our beliefs, and the beliefs holding you back are really just a product of the glasses we choose to look through. There really isn't any objectivity then to our perceptions because we are constantly modifying them to fit in with the assumptions we carry. What is visible to us really is a version of what is real modified to fit into our reality.

What Is Your Condition(ing)?

We are being conditioned before we can say "ma-ma." By the time we realize how we are conditioned, it's impossible to completely undo the process. But it can be improved and re-wired. My guess is most of us do not even stop and evaluate what our conditioning is. Even if we decide to do nothing about it, at least understanding why we are predisposed to behave certain ways is helpful and important. Let's look at how our conditioning is created.

Experience in our life is the first contributor to our conditioning. Everyone has specific incidents that occurred in their life which have a direct, significant impact on how they behave in the future. A high school teenager is involved in a tragic automobile accident where their friend dies at the scene. This experience will significantly mold the development of this young adult. The subsequent conditioning is not prescribed as positive or negative, that is up to the individual. But the severity of the situation heightens the impact on their life.

The second major contributor to our conditioning is what we heard when we were young. This is commonly known as verbal conditioning. What did you hear about yourself? What were you told about your future, your dreams, your potential? Tiger Woods' father, Earl Woods, apparently told Tiger that winning was the only option. By coaching Tiger with this attitude along with a gentle, fatherly love, it should come as no surprise that Tiger is one of the most accomplished athletes in history. He was told over and over there is only one place, first place.

Modeling is the third vital part of our conditioning. What did we see? How was life modeled to us? How were we shown how to move through life or deal with various circumstances, people, or ourselves? Were we shown life as a struggle? Were good decisions modeled for us? A young boy watches his father courageously start up a family business. This entrepreneurial spirit is welcomed and copied by the young man who eventually takes over the family business and becomes a successful businessman. No surprise, right? What he saw acted out, he inherently adopted into his own behavior.

We all are conditioned. Some have the luxury of receiving better care than others. Despite those differences, we all are assumed the responsibility to navigate through our own waters and decide which conditioning we wish to keep and which behaviors we will choose to change. However, don't you agree that it is unacceptable and a serious mistake on our parts to live without coming to some comprehension of our conditioning?

No.....Not Me

When confronted with the idea of having a "fear of success," many people quickly dismiss it based on the obvious paradox. As odd as a fear of success may sound, it is far more common than we think.

Accompanying success are many extra pressures, demands, and beliefs. In order for any success to continue, consistent effort needs to be applied. Success is not found in the mundane activities of our life, but when we explore and act toward attaining new challenges. Therefore, success is created when we stretch out, look and find new power in ourselves.

**If you are not used to or don't expect success,
it might be difficult to keep once you obtain it.**

The following are concrete examples of what fear of success might look like:

- You don't believe that you deserve all the good things and recognition that come your way.
- You fear being honored and/or recognized.
- Once you attain successful results, you don't feel you could sustain the same activity or results.
- You unknowingly trip yourself up, so you never attain a certain level of success.

Here are some common belief patterns of people who have bought into the fear of success:

- Will people like me if I make it to the top? I know they care about me now, when I am down.
- How do I know that I will be happy if I hit new goals, since I have never experienced happiness before?
- No matter what I do, it will never be enough. Being successful is an insatiable quest.
- The world is full of more talented people. I don't really deserve it.
- I am more comfortable when the world is a struggle and things are hard.

Optimist or Pessimist?

A couple encounters a difficult situation, such as an argument, a lay-off, or an illness. The husband reacts to the situation with despair, negative anxiety, and catastrophic predictions. Will we die? Are we going to divorce? Am I going to be unemployed? As a result of the impending pressures from those thoughts, his immunity decreases and he becomes sick. He then misses work due to his illness, and depression begins to kick in.

Conversely, the wife looks at the same scenario completely different. She sees setbacks for what they are, a temporary setback an inconvenience. Although she is not excited about the circumstances, she puts herself back in "order" and decides to move forward, taking control of what is in her realm of influence.

Everything only has the meaning we give it.

Pessimists tend to believe that negative circumstances will last for a long time and that the event is their fault. Dealing with the same issue, optimists take the misfortune and deal with it in an entirely different way. They see setbacks as temporary. They make it in isolated incident in only one part of their life. Give an optimist adversity, and they will try harder.

In testing thousands of people, Seligman found that a high number of us carry pessimistic attitudes, or at least carry tendencies towards pessimism. The next time you experience any inconvenience, listen to the conversation you have with yourself. How well did you deal with it?

The good news for pessimists is you can escape. Being a pessimist does not have to mean a life sentence to negative thinking. One can develop new thought patterns, which can lead to a more optimistic attitude.

Real pessimism isn't permanent, while true optimism is priceless.

Recent research shows that developing and sustaining an optimistic outlook carries many positive attributes such as living longer, enjoying healthier relationship, and attaining more fulfilling experiences.

Remember, healthy optimism is not saying everything is okay, when it really isn't. Operating with a healthy dose of optimism is when we have the ability to be hopeful, to see the positives in situations, and to deal with adversity in a proactive manner, where challenges do not force us to self destruct.

**A pessimistic attitude is only permanent
if you make it so.**

What's Your Explanatory Style?

Explanatory style is a psychological term that details how people explain to themselves why they are experiencing a certain event, either positive or negative. Seligman classified explanatory style into three parts.

Personal – people experience an event, and they either look at it internally or externally. Someone who looks at it internally would say, "I always forget my rain jacket," as opposed to an external reason such as, "That rain always sneaks up on me."

Permanent – People see the situation as permanent or unchangeable. Someone is rejected by a mate, and they say, "I will never find love again," instead of "that just wasn't meant to be."

Pervasive – People may see the situation affecting all areas of life. You make a mistake at work, and your response is, "I can't do anything right," versus "I won't make that mistake at work next time."

A pessimistic attitude feeds helplessness, while an optimistic attitude negates it.

When one indulges themselves in pessimism and couples that with personal and permanent statements, the culminating results are devastating. They are laying the groundwork to develop a helpless attitude for a very long time. Even worse, Seligman has strongly concluded that this recipe is almost a sure bet for depression.

What Messages Is Your Brain Playing?

Despite the amazing advances scientists have made studying the human body, they are only scratching the surface in learning the intricacies of the human brain. The amount of information our minds store is infinite. What's even more astonishing is how much data is stored that we aren't aware is there.

Our brain has been recording information since the day we were conceived. But our brain is way more high tech than any tape recorder we have ever seen. What happens is every experience we have encountered is recorded. Along with that experience, our brain also records how we felt. Our brain then records the experience and the feeling that accompanied it. That is why sometimes we feel an inexplicable feeling when we have a certain experience. Many times, our choices are based on a response to a past feeling which could lead to poor decision making in the present. If our brain then is telling us how we feel based on past feelings, we must be careful in making present choices.

**You will never be able to help yourself or others
if you are bound to your past.**

You need to be alert to what tape recorded messages your brain is sending you from past feelings you have associated with experiences. These thoughts and feelings are locked deep in your brain and might be scary to look at. But today's choices are too important to compromise. Listen to your tapes and be aware of what they are saying. Erase the tape's and create new recordings!

Time For Some Gardening

The stadium is packed full of people. Standing room only. A once in a lifetime opportunity has presented itself for the lucky few who were selected by a lottery to attend. Each person in attendance has a chance to exchange their set of problems for someone else's. Every person writes all of their troubles down on a sheet of paper. At once, they all throw their crumpled ball of paper onto the field. Then, everyone has a chance to read everybody's list and either inherit that person's problems or keep their own. One by one, each person excitedly runs to the field and hastily reads every list, presuming they will find that one list which would make life easy. Confused and dismayed, not one person exchanged their list for another's. After seeing what others are dealing with, each person decided they would rather live with their own problems than inherit another's.

We aren't privy to much of what goes on in other's lives. But, it is completely naïve for us to believe that any person living on this earth does not endure challenges, hard times, and stresses. No one has an "easy" button. Some may work through their tough times with more elegance, but everyone is equally vulnerable to life's disappointments.

Growing up, my dad must have wished for a better "weed puller." I would often see him going back over the areas I just finished. He had to constantly remind me, "Make sure and get the root!" In my zeal to complete my chores so I could play, I would take the quickest route, just pulling whatever came up, leaving the most important, yet invisible part, the root. What happened as a result? The same weed would pop up next week because the root was still in the ground.

"Those who think they have not time for bodily exercise will sooner or later have to find time for illness."
Edward Stanley

If I would have taken just a bit more time and went for the root my work would have been so much easier. Instead my Saturday chores would consist of having to pull the same weeds, week after week, until I pulled the root. Our lives are those weeds. As you deal with life, so many choices are the results of the old weeds we have let grow. Instead of pulling them out by the root, we pluck them off the top. They just resurface in time. We might not see them for a bit, but without addressing the root, eventually it will resurface.

In dealing with our "weeds," taking shortcuts become longcuts.

Strengths & Weaknesses

If someone were to ask you to "tell me some of your strengths and weaknesses," what would you say? I can rattle off my strengths for days, but when it comes to identifying, acknowledging, and working on weaknesses, it's a different story. It could be we don't want to admit them or that we just don't know they exist.

The truth is we don't like to look at or acknowledge our weaknesses, so most of us don't know them! How do we expect to get better in life if we haven't detailed where we want to improve?

I have set up the following guidelines for myself which has helped me deal with my strengths and weaknesses more honestly and effectively:

Strengths: I always strive to build on them. My inherent strengths won't go away, but I will need to continue cultivating them in order to keep building on what I have worked to develop. Continue to build on my successes, entrench them in my life. My strengths are my unique contribution to others. As the saying goes:

**We were born originals
so we will not die a copy!**

Weaknesses: Work on small improvements. My weaknesses might never become strengths, but I can improve on them so they are not a weakness, maybe considered neutral. Be realistic with myself and what I can achieve. Identify which weaknesses are going to remain that way and which ones I will improve.

Pike Syndrome

Researchers put a Northern Pike in a large aquarium. In the middle of the aquarium, they inserted a glass divider. On the other side of this glass partition was Thanksgiving dinner for the pike – minnows. As you might guess, the pike made several attempts to get at the minnows, endlessly battering its head against the glass wall. Finally, after numerous futile attempts, the pike gave up.

A few days later, the glass partition was removed. What does the pike do? The pike continued to swim only on the side of the aquarium it THOUGHT was open. Dinner was just a millimeter away!

It is easy to sympathize with the pike as it bangs its head on the glass until persistence loses to a bad headache. The lesson though, is that we ignore differences, we assume we know, our reactions become generalized, we have rigid commitments to past behaviors and beliefs, and we refuse to consider new alternatives. All of those result in us not maximizing our potential.

Doc, I think I have a case of Excusitis

An excuse is only bad if you decide to believe it.

I got onto a kick a couple years back where hearing excuses from others really annoyed me. I didn't have the self awareness to realize that I was way worse than the people irritating me. Once I determined that I had the biggest problem, I began to monitor how many excuses I made. Boy, was I surprised. I considered myself a person of action, not excuses. But here I was, throwing them out like trash!

Permitting ourselves to make excuses allows us to avoid taking responsibility.

I found as I cut down on my excuses I experienced more responsibility, more ownership of my life. For me, that responsibility equated to a healthy confidence and a more proactive attitude.

Take a look at people who are "going places." Don't you think they could make the same excuses as people going nowhere? You bet! People who are on the right track in life tend to use less excuses, while the people who are going nowhere fast will have a book of reasons why they are where they are.

It's not a coincidence that people who have success are not full of excuses, is it? My money says that if you were to listen carefully to people who are struggling, you would hear a thousand of them.

"He that is good for making excuses is seldom good for anything else."
Benjamin Franklin

Excuses are like bad habits. The more you fertilize and water them, the deeper their roots grow. Let's take a common example I hear when I work with professional sales people. "But, Mark, when I grew up I..." Don't get me wrong. I am sympathetic to the circumstances that you experienced, and I am sorry you had to go through anything painful. However, the more you use that excuse as justification for not maximizing your abilities, the harder it will become to get what you want. Please understand what I am saying here. I am not discrediting one's past at all. What I am challenging us to do is examine where our excuses are, take ownership of them, and see where they are holding us back. We lose out on the opportunity to get rid of or change them if we never become aware of their existence.

Money, Money, Money

Any time we spend money it is a choice. If you are like me, you could relate how you spend money to many of the reasons in chapter three, which discusses why we make the choices we do.

Every person reading this book is completely unique in their choices. We are also unique in personality. Each one of us wants to utilize our choices to show our uniqueness. Money is a huge contributor to how we can exercise that right; it's called expressive value.

Expressive value is how we choose to show the world who we are.

Sometimes, expressing ourselves becomes so important that it overruns our ability to think rationally, and it can even distort us into spending money we don't have. As shocking as it sounds, people will put their future at risk in order to make sure they express their value.

I had a friend who drove a very nice Mercedes. I didn't know how much money they made, but based on their car, I figured they must be making a decent salary. At lunch one day, this individual began complaining about money. He went on to tell me he had accrued an enormous amount of debt. In addition, he had high insurance costs and could barely afford to make the payments on their car. So, why would this person with huge amounts of financial restrictions continue to buy this car? They told me in so many words. Expressing themselves as wealthy was more important than being financially comfortable at that time.

Not all money is about expressing ourselves, but it is a trap we easily fall prey to. Expressing ourselves with our money seems to become more excessive with the more money we make too.

Well, if you are similar to 99.9% of the world, you will have fallen victim to what is called Parkinson's Law. Parkinson's Law states that people's spending is equal to their income. The more money we make, the more money we spend. We just can't delay our gratification! We get money, and we find things we just HAVE to have. Isn't it funny how quickly our "have to haves" pop up only once we know we can afford them?

Adaptation, the inability to delay gratification, and giving ourselves logical explanations in order to justify, all play a serious role in why we are guilty of Parkinson's Law. Money is a sensitive issue for many, and it will continue to be as long as people are emotionally fueled. We always have a choice what we buy and when we buy it. Monitor your spending habits to see if what you are spending in the present is potentially hurting your future.

Time Keeps On Slippin', Slippin' Slippin'
Into the Future

I kept procrastinating going back to school. A friend whom I had told I would start earlier asked me why I had not enrolled. Being afflicted with an extreme case of excusitis, I replied, "I just don't have the time." Come on. Of course I had the time. I just had not chosen to use it to go back to school.

Over the past few years I have begun to take a much more serious look at how I use my time. I know that I have the same amount of time as those I admire. In terms of time, I had to come to grips with the truth that I had the same resources of time as everyone. How were they able to accomplish those things? How did they do it? One thing I finally had to admit: we have the same amount of time.

**We all have 24 hours every day to spend
however we wish.**

I was such a poor steward of my time that at one point I even had a TV schedule. Isn't that sick? That didn't begin to change until I realized how much television I was watching. First, I had to know how much I was really watching, not how much I *thought* I was watching. The only accurate way was to track in a notebook how much television I watched during a week. It was WAY too much.

What were other people doing with that same time? What were people that I admired doing while I was watching television? What could I be doing to help me get closer to becoming the person I wanted? After I swallowed a reality pill about my viewing habits, I came to a very simple but profound revelation:

I spend most of my time doing what I think feels best, *not* what is best.

Remember, we look to find what will feel the best for us now. We seek and crave finding pleasure. Of course, I am not going to elect going back to school versus watching 24 or Soprano's. I had to look past my current feeling and admit to myself that every hour I spent doing something worth nothing was another hour farther away I was to attaining something I truly wanted.

We have the time for whatever we want. The truth is we don't want to TAKE the time to do it, otherwise we would.

"But I have a stressful full time job," we say. Wake up 15 minutes earlier. Take half of your lunch break. Put aside an hour on Saturday and Sunday. From just those suggestions alone, you would have 6 more hours of time per week to invest in yourself. What are the possibilities if you decide to dedicate those 6 hours to pursuing bettering yourself?

> *"There's a myth that time is money.*
> *In fact, time is more precious than money.*
> *It's a nonrenewable resource.*
> *Once you've spent it, and if you've spent it*
> *badly, it's gone forever."*
> Neil Fiore

Look, I know life throws curveballs. I am in the same batter's box as you! I am in no way insinuating that you should never watch television, "veg out," or take alone time. Just realize you have a choice with your time. If you aren't where you want to be in any area of life, there IS time available to you to do what you want. You must choose to take that time as your own.

> *"Time is the most valuable*
> *thing a man can spend."*
> Theophrastus

Anti-Inertia Challenge

Where are you fighting with yourself between wants and willingness?

Are you sacrificing honesty in order to stay mentally aligned?

What do your life results tell you regarding your choices?

How can you be a better friend to yourself?

What's your favorite excuse? How are you going to stop using it?

What roots do you have that are still in "the ground?"

List your major strengths and weaknesses. Confirm your list with a close friend or family member you trust.

List three improvements you will make with your time.

CHANGE YOUR CHOICES
CHANGE YOUR LIFE

Understand the power in choice. Realize you can harness that power to create your life.

Our lives are a predictable result of a cycle we unknowingly exercise constantly.

There is a "why" behind every choice we make.

Truly understanding ourselves is an essential aspect of choice making.

Choices are governed by universal laws. We need to be aware how they work in order to grasp their impact.

Specific behaviors differentiate people who live in fulfillment versus those who don't.

We all deal with adversity. How we choose to deal with it is the critical factor.

Choosing to exercise courage, discipline, a positive attitude, and persistence are vital to our choice making foundation.

Choice making becomes clear after we identify our desired outcome and detail specific steps to get there.

Chapter Five

LAWS GOVERNING CHOICE

*There are predictable, consistent laws
that will always accompany choice.*

Law #1:
The Results Of Our Choices Won't Always
Match Up With Our Intentions

During the winter of 2001, I was living in New Jersey. Being born and raised in Southern California, it is appropriate to say I was "barely surviving" a typical winter in the East. I returned home to sunny California for a quick respite. The temperature outside was around 15 degrees when I returned to New Jersey. But something didn't feel right as I entered my home. Finally it hit me. The temperature didn't change at all when I walked into my house. My heart dropped. I ran over to the heating thermostat and looked at the digital thermostat. It read *26 degrees*. At that moment, I don't know if I was more apprehensive about seeing if I could fix the heater without blowing my house up or trying to sleep in a house that was below freezing. Being barely qualified to use a hammer, I wasn't feeling very confident in my chances at fixing the problem. I went to the basement, walking as if I knew exactly what I was doing, and did exactly what I thought I would do. I circled around the heater and reluctantly admitted, "I have no idea what is wrong."

"Okay, Mark, time to get creative," I pondered as I began to feel sleepy. I then came up with the brilliant idea that I would bring all of my blankets into the living room, build a huge fire, and sleep cozily all night. "So," I thought, "What can I use to make the biggest and longest lasting fire possible?" As my handyman genius began to rev, I saw exactly what I needed. My solution was a big, thick phone book. With the phone book in hand, I ran back into the living room with all six layers of clothes still on. I prepped the fireplace. All ready to go. I could imagine the radiating warmth already. I struck the match to the phone book expecting to see a fire ball light up the room.

A teeny small cloud of dark gray smoke emitted from the fireplace. Needing heat quicker, I decided to light all four edges to get it going. Before I knew it, instead of a beautiful fire, I had a billowing cloud of smoke in the fireplace. "Well," I thought as I felt a spell of relief come over me, "at least I have the flume in the right position." Wrong. I was soon engulfed in a huge, black cloud of smoke. The phone book did not catch fire at all. It actually served as an ignitor for smoke! Panic began to set in as I didn't know what to do.

Something had to happen quick. The house was filling up with smoke. I had one of two options. Wait it out, or yeah, you guessed it, open up the windows! I didn't want my house smelling like a burned phone book, so I decided to open up all the windows. One minute passed and then another without much air movement. I turned on the fans. Twenty-six degrees in the house with the windows open and the fans were on. The temperature was definitely going in the wrong direction! After about a half hour the smoke finally dissipated out of the house. I plunked myself down on the couch thinking what I should do now.

I found myself on the way to Target to buy a space heater. Not a bad idea. I could use a space heater anytime during a winter this severe. My new plan was simple: go to Target, pick up the heater and return home and sleep. I was feeling confident with my new agenda.

I left Target just as it is closing. Upon arriving home, I took the space-heater out of the box, plugged it in, and while I was imagining warm air hitting my face, I instead felt a cold breeze. What? I pick up the unit and looked on the back to see what switch I missed. Nothing wrong there. I picked up the box. Oh, is it cold air because it says "fan" on the box? I could not believe it! I felt like the biggest idiot on earth. Not only did I buy a fan, but by the time I got home, Target was closed.

I immediately called every hotel in a 20 mile radius. No hotel would give me a room for less than $150. I remembered seeing a local place down the road I thought would be my best bet. It was already almost 11:00, and I would be waking up in a couple hours anyway. I walked up to the window, paid my money and then saw a sign on the wall which fittingly ends this story. The sign read: "$75 per hour."

What's the lesson in all of this? Throughout the whole night, every choice I made was backed by good intentions. Every decision was geared toward heating my house so I could sleep. But ironically, despite my greatest intentions, the results of my choices only made my situation worse and my night more difficult to deal with.

Regardless of intent, our choices will not always produce the results we expect.

Choices do not care about intentions, and sometimes, regardless of where our heart is, our choices do not turn out the way we expected.

Law #2
One Strike and You Are Out!

You decide you are going to be more complimentary to your spouse. For days you make a conscious effort to sincerely compliment them. One day you come home from a long, exhaustive day at work--one of those days we would like to forget. Without thinking, you snap a derogatory comment that is cunning and hurtful. Before the words are out of your mouth, you realize you made a mistake, but it's too late.

A number of good choices can be wiped out with one bad choice.

That one statement will negate every positive step you took for the past several days. It can virtually erase all of the momentum from all of the previous compliments. Only one little statement has the power to delete weeks of positive communication. It only takes one bad choice to ruin a number of good ones.

Law #3
What's Done Is Done

On certain days, I really crave a fast food meal even though I know there are thousands of healthier alternatives available.

I give in to my temptations and go chow down a burger and fries like it is my first meal in months. After finishing, I regretfully think about all the things I can do to work off the bad food. I'll exercise more tomorrow, or I'll eat a whole mess of fruit, or no more soda for a month. The problem? I already ate the food.

There are choices you make where the effect can be reversed but not without sacrificing time. For instance, say I buy a shirt that I like in red. When I get home and show it to my wife (the fashion police), she reminds me that it is against "Fashion Law" for me to wear red. I return to the store and exchange it for a blue one (which is acceptable). In this case, yes, the effect is changeable, but my original action is never reversible.

Other choices are impacted more severely by this law. The consequences are far more detrimental. A young, dating couple decides to have intercourse. She gets pregnant. They will both be parents before being able to legally drink. A couple years down the road, they divorce and the child is raised in chaos and instability. Unfortunately for this couple, they can't go back. What's done is done. There are no exchanges. Although they love their child, the consequences of their single choice will remain with them and their child for as long as they live.

Law #4
The Law of Accumulation

You look in the mirror one day and surprisingly realize you are well over your ideal weight. "How did this happen?" you scream. Every day you decide to put your loose change in a jar. When you come home you drop in amounts of change that seem inconsequential at the time. However, a year later, your jar is full. You cash it out and you have $100. In our lifetime we will experience many situations that exactly replicate the examples above. When we do, we are experiencing the Law of Accumulation which states that:

"We must not, in trying to think about how we can make a big difference, ignore the small daily differences we can make which, over time, add up to big differences that we often cannot foresee." Marian Edelman

Not exercising as much, eating poorly, or snacking on unhealthy foods would all be logical factors as to how weight could pile on without us realizing it. Slowly, hundreds or thousands of small decisions kept culminating, little by little, until you noticed the results. Why does this happen? Because we don't think small choices matter.

The sum of many small cumulative choices is bigger and has more effect than any single choice could ever be.

The smaller the choice, the less we think about it. "Nah, this bag of peanut M&M's won't hurt me," you say. You're right. The one bag will not hurt you. What will hurt you is when you buy into that lie every day for a year. Choices are sneaky. They stay behind the scenes while they take time to develop speed and then WHAM!

Choices are deceptive because
the consequences are not instant.

Every little choice we make DOES add up. There aren't many choices that carry no significance. There are choices more serious in nature, while others are or seem trivial; but be aware because the law of accumulation is sneakily, slowly, and deliberately collecting its ammunition. One day, it will give you back what it has collected.

"Remember the law of accumulation:
The sum of many little collaborative
efforts isn't little."
Michael Nolan

Law #5
Choice Has A Short-Term Memory

Anytime, anyplace, we can decide to do anything we want. We can start making new or different decisions at anytime, no matter what choices we have made in our past! Within the unlimited boundaries of choice, lies the ability to begin new and fresh any time.

I don't care what your past has been.
Your future is spotless.

We've all had those times where it feels like every choice we make is wrong. But no matter how many bad decisions we make in a row, we have a new start with our next choice.

Say you have a poor history in dating selections. After another dating calamity, you resolve to never date again. Every person you pick is wrong. Well, choice doesn't care about your past record. All choice is concerned with is your next choice. Who or how you decide is your call. But your slate is clean with choice!

We always have the power to start new, fresh. Our past is done, and the decisions we made are over. The consequences still remain, but the future is wide open to the possibilities of new choices.

Law #6
Choices Are Graded On A Curve

Here's a rule I tell my friends regarding stock investing. Buy whatever stock I sell, and sell whatever stock I buy. It seems like no matter what choice I make it is the wrong one! No one is immune to making the wrong choice. At times, it is easy to live under a false pretense that every choice we make should work out perfectly or how we planned. But choices in life just don't operate that way. All you can do is make the best choice you know to make and let the chips fall.

We will never be perfect in the choices we make. Don't expect that out of yourself. You will only experience frustration and reinforce bad beliefs. No one makes the right choice 100% of the time. All we can do once our choice is made is be confident we did our best with the resources available to us, and that whatever happens, we will choose to react proactively and positively.

Law #7
Will It Get Better Or Worse?

I was in a black world of misery and destruction knowing my former wife was sleeping with another man. I was headed downhill, fast. You know the expression, "Get your head out of the sand?" I wanted to find a hole and bury my head as quickly and as deep as I could. In fact, many days I did exactly that. What I didn't think about though, was that by putting my head in the sand I didn't do anything but perpetuate my problem. My pain was so severe I didn't want to look at it. I thought it was easier to try and push it away. But choosing to pretend I wasn't in tremendous pain only worked against me because the sixth law of choice says:

Will it get better or worse? Yes, it will.

How we work to resolve our circumstances is completely up to us. The scenarios we face will either get better or worse. Time doesn't afford us "life time outs." While I was sulking up a storm, my personal life was going the wrong way. Everything we are involved in is constantly getting better or worse. Which one? That's up to us and what action we take. This is another example of where choice seems so unforgiving, so cold. It can feel so defeating when we feel beaten down and we can't catch our breath. We want to put life on pause just for a day. Life can feel so confining that even our breathing can feel restricted. Be that as it may, life is always moving, and in the direction of the choices we make. Will your situation get better or worse? Yes, it will. You decide.

Law #8
Control = Expectations

Isn't it fascinating that prearranged marriages have a higher success rate than unarranged marriages? I was perplexed by that statistic until I came across this interesting observation. The seventh law of choice says:

The more control you have over the choice, the higher the expectation on the result.

As Americans, we have complete control over who we marry. Since we have the ultimate choice, we then bring the ultimate expectation with it. Our expectation is directly commensurate with the amount of control we had in the decision. Aren't unmet expectations one of the most common reasons couples drift apart? Of course, because they had complete control and their level of expectation matched it.

A broke college student desperately needs a car but does not have the financial resources to buy one. Their necessity far outweighs any other factor, and they just need a car. One day, a friend comes to them and says, "Hey look, I got an old clunker I could give you. Do you want it?" They take it. Since they didn't have any other options, there really wasn't much choice here except take it or leave it. Given that the control level was so minimal, the expectation level will reciprocate. The expectation will be low! Picture yourself in this scenario. You would have so little expectation with the car. Why? Because you had such minimal control in the choice.

Law #9
You Reap What You Sow

> *"Nobody ever did or ever will escape*
> *the consequences of their choices."*
> Montaport

We are all familiar with the phrase 'cause and effect.' A word that describes cause and effect accurately is causality. Causality is defined as the relationship between an event, which is the cause, and a second event, which is the effect. The second is always a result of the first.

For every choice we make there is an outcome.

Outcomes can be positive, negative, or indifferent. EVERY choice we make has an effect associated with it. The quality of your health, relationships, beliefs, state of life, and occupation are all involved in a cause and effect relationship.

After years of trouble, Nancy's son, Mike had finally decided to turn his life around. Drugs, theft, incarceration, and life on the streets were beginning to take their toll. Ravaged by living this defeated life, Mike decided that he wanted to leave life on the streets and start new. Nancy knew that poor credit, no work history, and a police record would make finding decent employment difficult. Shortly after, though, Mike landed a job working a line shift position at a local fast food restaurant. After a month of diligent, hard work, he was up for a promotion and extremely excited at both the potential financial rewards and the new found personal success. But Mike didn't consider that the restaurant required mandatory background checks for any employee being promoted. Unfortunately, Mike's past record was reviewed, and he no longer had any chance to attain the promotion.

My immediate response is occupied by sentiments of unfairness and pity for Mike. However, that is in our world of emotion. The universal laws of choice do not bend. Emotion is non-existent. Despite Mike's great progress and changed behaviors, his past was inescapable. Those choices he made would always be there. The most difficult part of this law is that your current life can be 180 degrees from the time when you made a choice, yet, your past choices still remain.

Your current behavior doesn't erase your past

What can we take from this? First, realize that in the choices we make, the consequences will remain with us for the rest of our life. They might not always come back to haunt us, but they will always be there. Two, when these consequences reveal themselves to you at a later time, understand this is part of a natural law and you will need to move on, around, or through.

For Mike, it is not that since he made bad choices he will never have opportunities again. That is not the case. What does hold true is that choices made in the past and the subsequent consequences will accompany us as we move through life. And at times unknown to us, these consequences may hurt our present condition. I once had a friend say to me they felt they were "being penalized for their past." In essence, we are and we can be. We can be penalized for our past sins at any time and for as long as we live. Is this fair? Unfortunately, that is irrelevant because the ,consequences don't consider fairness. We must understand the reality and be ready to face the fire when it arises despite how unfair it seems.

Law #10
Anyone Want To Play Domino's?

Take the major parts of your life. Things like health, spirituality, emotional well being, work, home, etc. Taken at face value, these dimensions seem separate, but at a deeper level they are closely interconnected. Law #10 states that:

Choices you make in one area of your life will affect other areas too.

In an effort to ride an economic downturn, your company has to maintain current salary levels. This news hits you hard, especially with a second child on the way. Anticipating the future with a shortage of cash adds tremendous stress to your relationship. As a result of your employment conditions you and your spouse begin to disagree more as finances become a worry for both of you. Aside from your work and home life being negatively affected, your physical body also begins to feel the effects. Your mood is more negative, and you start to slip into moments of mild depression. Along with your relationship, work, and health, your spirituality begins to fade along with the rest of your life. The cycle goes on. It all started at work and shortly invades all aspects of our lives. There is no separating it. We don't have the ability to segregate the parts; they are interconnected.

Law #11
Choice Offers Deceptive Flexibility Plans

You accumulated some major debt and are hoping for some relief. You have a glimpse of hope when you receive a piece of mail from a credit card company. "Exciting offer for select individuals only" it states. "For a limited time only, receive 0% finance charges when you open an account with us." Bingo! You sign up excited that you see a way out of your financial hole. Six months later you receive a statement. Your stomach is suddenly in the back of your throat. An additional $411.42 appears on the bill. In disbelief you call customer service. A friendly but uncaring representative says, "I am sorry, Mr. Williams, you had 0% interest for the first six months; after that your APR is 24%."

Our freedom to choose is exactly the same. Initially, we make a choice. We don't feel any consequences and can't see any in the near future. Then, out of nowhere, we are hit with the outcome, the hard reality.

Here is a fascinating paradox about choice. When it comes to choosing, we have the ultimate freedom. We can always choose. Rarely do we come across choices in life that are so dire we really don't "have" a choice. For the majority of our lives, we live in a total freedom of choosing whatever we want.

Our freedom to choose is deceiving because all of our accountability comes after the fact, and that can occur when we least expect it.

Like the credit card, when we make choices, sometimes we have a six month grace period with no penalties. We think we hit the jackpot, then out of nowhere come nasty ramifications. Without any idea, we get hit with huge APR's we never expected! The paradox lies in the fact that, despite this perfect freedom we have to make choices, the accountability is so restricting. There is no flexibility with the consequences of our choices despite us having the ultimate ability to choose.

Have you seen the dog leash that can stretch for yards so the dog can roam, but when the owner wants the dog to stop, they push a button on the leash and the dog stops in their tracks? Our lives are the same way. Life is walking us with a flexible leash that gives us tons of freedom to walk, smell, and run. But when we don't expect it, just like a dog running wild in the grass, we can get yanked back when our leash is pulled back. When we experience this it is humbling, and once again we are reminded of choice, and that despite its wondrous freedom, accountability will someday follow.

Anti-Inertia Challenge

Identify a time when you experienced each law of choice:

1. Results didn't match with intentions

2. One strike and you're out!

3. What's done is done

4. Law of Accumulation

5. Choices have short-term memory

6. Choices are graded on a curve

7. Will it get better or worse?

8. **Expectation is equal to the amount of control**

9. **Reap what you sow**

10. **Domino effect**

11. **Deceptive flexibility plan**

CHANGE YOUR CHOICES CHANGE YOUR LIFE

Understand the power in choice. Realize you can harness that power to create your life.

Our lives are a predictable result of a cycle we unknowingly exercise constantly.

There is a "why" behind every choice we make.

Truly understanding ourselves is an essential aspect of choice making.

Choices are governed by universal laws. We need to be aware how they work and grasp their impact.

> **Specific behaviors differentiate people who live in fulfillment versus those who don't.**

We all deal with adversity.
How we choose to deal with it is the critical factor.

Choosing to exercise courage, discipline, a positive attitude, and persistence are vital to our choice making foundation.

Choice making becomes clear after we identify our desired outcome and detail specific steps to get there.

Chapter Six

PURSUER OR STRUGGLER?

Pursuers take what they have and make more of it;
strugglers blame the world for what they have.

Which Are You?

Struggler   Contenter   Pursuer

Strugglers: This group of people have hard lives. They can never seem to get over the proverbial "top." Everyday is a monumental chore filled with desperation, negativity, excuses, criticism, and climbing uphill. The struggler is that person who can never seem to catch a break up, who tells you all of the things against them. They are the people who you feel bad for. Strugglers can never find the right job and find life hard to view life as enjoyable.

Contenters are people who live in the middle. They do not yearn for the things of a pursuer, yet they do not complain about where they are at, like a struggler. They are simply content with what they have and do not need anything more. This contentment does not mean wanting or pursuing more is negative; it only means that contenters are happy with what they have and do not complain about what they don't have.

Pursuers are those people who make it happen. They are the group of people who have what most others want. This isn't exclusive to money. Pursuers have happy and fulfilling relationships, they are happy in their own skin, they have goals, ambition and are always looking for more. When you meet a pursuer, you know it. They have a magnetic charisma that we want to be a part of. They won't make an excuse; they will make a way.

Pursuers and strugglers want the same things. Pursuers get them because they are willing to pay the price—a price strugglers aren't willing to pay.

My experience has shown me that most people are either a struggler or a pursuer. Fear, shame, beliefs, and other factors create people into believing they are content, and some truly are. Our focus will center on people who fall into either the struggler or pursuer camp. There are people who fall on the extreme sides of either group, or there are some who blend in both, depending on what part of life we are referencing. For instance, we might be very well off financially, so we immediately assume we are a pursuer, not a struggler. But we are full of complaints, so in that aspect, we are a struggler.

It will be easy to convince ourselves we are not strugglers, but maybe we are in certain areas. If you are like me, you are not a complete struggler, but you are a struggler in certain areas. Whatever it is, identify the areas of "struggle" and work to strengthen them. Once someone buys into the pursuer way, it is rare to see them become a struggler. However, I do often see strugglers become pursuers.

People who have experienced the worst life has to offer still make choices that allow them to live the life of a pursuer. In fact, many of the strongest pursuers I know are the people who have the right to be the lowest struggler. Just because we were dealt a lousy hand does not automatically convict us to live it out.

How Much Does That "Different" Cost?

Given their dire circumstances, strugglers badly want things to be different. Funny thing, I haven't heard many of them admit they understand why they struggle. Yes, many of them made their own bed, but that doesn't mean they enjoyed living with one difficulty after another. Life is not supposed to be lived that way. Here's the problem strugglers have:

Strugglers aren't willing to pay the price for different.

It is much easier for strugglers to complain than to take hard, disciplined action. Remember back in chapter three we learned why we make the choices we do and we discussed the weighted scale? The scale tips much more favorably toward the pain one is enduring in their current reality because it seems comfortable and easier than the pain of changing one's reality in order to get "different." Even though making changes would seem blatantly obvious, the comfort of their norm overrides the pain of trying new.

Life would be so much easier for strugglers if they would readily admit that they are not willing to do what it takes to make their life different.

I worked with an older gentlemen, Pat, who sadly came across financial hardships. A few miscalculated choices compounded by bad breaks had put him in a difficult situation financially where he was "strapped." After paying the necessities, he wouldn't have much money left over, according to him. Whenever I saw Pat, he invariably would complain he had no money.

After a few months of watching this, I concluded that my hope to help Pat outweighed my fear of being nosy. I finally asked when an opportune time arose, "Do you have a budget?" "No," he replied. "Do you think that would help your situation?" I asked. "Yes," he responded. We discussed the benefits of a budget, and then I left it open to him. I told him whenever he was ready, I was more than happy to take as much time necessary to work with him. Guess what? He never asked and sadly never did a budget. Did his financial situation change? No. It stayed exactly the same, and so did his complaints.

If we were to ask Pat why he didn't do a budget, we would receive a myriad of answers. The truth? He wasn't willing to pay the price of being disciplined and responsible to do a budget. What do his actions say? Despite his verbal complaining, it told me he wasn't REALLY willing to pay the price necessary to change his financial situation.

Pursuers make change happen if they want it.

I am fortunate to know many people I consider pursuers, and I find it sad and ironic that pursuers are more likely to have budgets than strugglers. It should be the other way around. Surprisingly, that is not true.

If a pursuer wants different, the cost is irrelevant. They ARE willing to pay the price. A friend of mine once told me, "Mark, you are always willing to pay the price." That is true only when I WANT to or CHOOSE to. It is either pay the price or reap the consequences. I'll pay the price of different if I really want it.

Shhhh......I'm Talking To Myself

What one says when they talk to themselves is a major difference between strugglers and pursuers. You might be wondering if I ask people what they are telling themselves. I don't have to. What we do on a daily basis tells the world everything they need to know. In fact, anyone has the ability to know how we speak to ourselves because:

Our actions reveal exactly what is going on inside.

Most people talk a great game. I can talk with the best of them when it comes to pretending how great everything is or how amazingly ambitious I am. But, do you know where the truth lies? In our behavior.

Strugglers are communicating good intentions most of the time, saying they want so many things to be different, but their actions show that inside they are full of negative self talk and beliefs which derail them from moving forward. Have you ever listened to the conversations you have with yourself?

We live in such a cynical, selfish world. You better be your own best friend because we all feel like we are all alone sometimes. During those times in your life where you feel like no one is there, you better be able to comfort, love, and pick yourself up.

This world has enough critics; don't be your own.

Pursuers have a self talk that is real, but optimistic, challenging, but encouraging, and relentlessly pushing, yet compassionate. These conversations help keep the pursuer moving forward when the challenges come, while the inner conversations of a struggler serve as the killer of all possible positive change.

What's Your Hobby?

Collecting injustices is a favorite pastime for strugglers. "My boss didn't like me because...." "This company never gave me a chance after...." Pursuers don't pay attention to injustices because they hold them back. Strugglers like them because they are justifications and excuses for shunning responsibility. It gives them further evidence why they don't have what they think they want.

Brian was a typical struggler. He lived paycheck to paycheck but was never willing to put his actions ahead of his excuses. After not making as much money as he thought, I heard him say, "They totally taxed me." "That's funny, I got taxed, too," I replied. Knowing Brian was struggling financially, I offered Brian an incentive to make more money. I was blown away by his response, "The government will just tax me more." He was so caught up in collecting all of the reasons why the world was against him that he couldn't concentrate on doing good for himself! What is the major problem with operating this way?

Collecting injustices allows you to avoid responsibility.

Life isn't fair. Yes, like Brian, you might not get what you deserve. I know that is hard. We have all been passed up for a promotion we deserved. We have all seen others receive praise for a job we completed. Please GET OVER IT! Better yet, tell me how your collection of injustices has helped you. Don't look for reasons why the world is treating you unfairly. Rather, pursue the path toward releasing those feelings and moving toward it is what you want.

What Are You Attracting?

The law of attraction is the idea that you will inevitably attract into your life those things that are in line with your most dominant thoughts. When I was first introduced to this concept, I thought it was too "out there" for me until I began to look more closely at myself and others.

Take a look at a pursuer you know. Who are their friends? Are they other pursuers? Why is that? Probably because they are attracting other pursuers to them. Look at a struggler. Who does this person spend time with? We want to be with other people who are like us.

We attract what we ARE, not what we want.

After spending all day with a struggler, I feel exhausted. Being surrounded with a constant negative outlook is tiring. A sad but common irony I see in strugglers is that, because of deep-seeded negative beliefs, they unknowingly push people or things away because they feel undeserving. I hear strugglers complain all the time about how bad their relationships are. It has to be explained to them it is a result of either a belief that they don't deserve more or that is what they are attracting. Most often, it is a combination of both. Look at your friends, your relationships, your companions at work. Who are you attracting? Why are you attracting them? If you don't like your answers, do something to change them! The adage, "you are who your friends are" is as old as it is true. You might find that if you start spending time with pursuers, you will begin to see things differently.

401K? But I Have To Have This!

Pursuers take time to plan. They think about their future. They don't live in a perpetual cycle of "today, today, today." Conversely, strugglers tend to live as though each day was their last. They say they can't afford to invest in their 401K, but they can afford to buy a nice car. They dress in all the recent fashions. It's not that strugglers can't afford it, but that they haven't taken the time to plan for their future (remember delayed gratification?).

The cycle becomes a perpetual one for the struggler. They are never able to plan because they are living in a constant "fear of the present" danger zone. Living paycheck to paycheck will not resolve itself on its own. You have to plan a way out. This way of living in survival mode all the time makes them think they can never slow down to think about their lives six months, two years, five years, or ten years down the road.

So, what happens in five years? The struggler is in the same position, complaining about the same issues, saying they just don't have time to plan for the future.

Comfort Can Be Found In Chaos

People are more likely to remain in their negative "environment of comfort" if that is what they are used to than choose to be in an environment they would describe as positive.

Growing up I had a close friend, Steve, who lived in a very chaotic home environment. From physical abuse, to emotional abuse, to constant financial pressure, to parental neglect, he experienced it all. Time after time, Steve would verbalize his desire to have a tranquil life; a life where undue stresses, like having zero money, would cease to exist. But the future held a different sentiment. Unknown to Steve, he was more comfortable in a chaotic environment. That is what he was used to and, therefore, would easily revert back to. There were brief moments in time where Steve would faintly touch the life he thought he wanted, but it was too far out of his comfortable chaos. What I noticed in Steve was that his choices would continually create situations causing him to shift back into an environment that more closely resembled what he was used to, constant trouble.

Problems, extra stresses, and torn relationships all typically follow strugglers around because that is the environment they are comfortable with. As annoying and tiresome as their environment is, that is their "home." Twisted as it sounds, I have witnessed strugglers literally search out an environment that, despite its obvious negativities, won their heart. What we are used to will invariably win over new or better. What we are used to and want is comfort, despite the costs.

Pursuers have the ability to make their comfort zone not being in one.

Pursuers find their comfort in their successes. They find their comfort in growth, learning, achieving, ambition, and fulfilled goals. In relation to their comfort zones, consider this as well when looking at strugglers and pursuers:

Comfort zones are what people revert back to and live in, not what they want.

Strugglers can't find their comfort zone because, although they are struggling in it, they do not want to be there and will not acknowledge their rut.

"That's Just My Luck….."

A sales professional, Susanne, was hoping to find her way through a difficult season. Positive momentum just seemed so hard to come by. We were together talking strategy, and we began discussing a lead that went sour. I offered to call the prospect, hoping to show Susanne how she could do what it is I was asking her to do.

After a very effective call, Susanne sheepishly commented, "Ha, that is just your luck." She was quickly reminded that the results had nothing to do with luck. The success was a result of practice, failing, successes, and studying sales. I told her I have done that millions of times. There was nothing lucky about it! I am not in a position to coach sales because of luck. But isn't it funny that the first thing the struggler attributed to another's success was luck?

> *"People are always blaming their circumstances for what they are. I don't believe in circumstances. The people who get on in this world are the people who get up and look for the circumstances they want, and, if they can't find them, make them."*
> *George Shaw*

Strugglers would like to believe they are handpicked by life to have bad things happen to them. They almost flatter themselves by believing all the bad luck only happens to them.

Out driving while cold calling, we approached a yellow light. The driver pounded on the brakes, and the car came to a screeching halt. "Chicken!" I jokingly screamed. "Yeah, knowing my luck, a cop would have been there." I laughed it off, but I had heard this individual make comments in a similar fashion before. Although we made a joke of it, this person truly felt that way. Their life reflected this outlook as well. This individual was struggling in a unhealthy relationship, had serious family troubles, could not get their finances in order, and was having difficulty settling down in a job. This struggler genuinely felt handpicked by the "bad luck" gods from above.

Thomas Jefferson said it best when he said:

> *"I find the harder I work, the more luck I seem to have."*

Pursuers believe in luck as a consequence of the work they have put in. Yes, of course, there is "luck" in this world, but pursuers and strugglers view it totally differently. Strugglers think they have bad luck, while pursuers strive to make good luck. Plus, if it was quantifiable, who do you think would experience more "good luck"—a struggler or pursuer? Why? Because pursuers are making things happen, opening new doors, and creating relationships through others.

Struggler say "I can't because….."
Pursuers ask, "How can I?"

On the topic of luck, here is an interesting pattern I've observed. When strugglers experience something they would describe as "good luck" for someone else, they don't even acknowledge it! On the contrary, when pursuers have bad luck, they look at it as a temporary bad break that is a minor setback, and that's it.

Complaining = Not Changing

Have you ever noticed that people who choose to complain (besides they are strugglers) are rarely taking any positive action to correct the issue they are complaining about!

If you are willing to complain,
take the energy to change it.

Next time you hear someone complaining about their dead-end job ask them, "So, what are you doing about it?" After you weed out their excuses and stories I have a hunch what they are doing. The problem for strugglers is they are likely to complain and then do absolutely nothing about it.

How often do you hear pursuers complain? I know they do, but it is with much less frequency than strugglers. The reason is simple.

Pursuers will take action to change what they do not like.

Instead of complaining they are acting! They are thinking of ways they can change their current reality. They most certainly could invent excuses if they want to, but they choose not to.

"We can throw stones, complain about them, stumble on them, climb over them, or build with them."
William Ward

A co-worker came to me terrified they had no money left, payday was not for another week, and they had custody of their two children for the weekend. We took care of a short-term financial band aid, but I realized there was a much deeper issue many weeks prior. I asked this person what they were doing about being in such financial dire straits as this was not the first time I helped them out. Expecting to hear something that resembled a plan, I heard nothing but stories, fictional that is.

It was unfortunately very apparent that this individual, although willing to complain how bad finances were, was not willing to take any steps to alleviate the problem. I kindly offered this advice:

If you aren't going to do anything to change it, don't complain about it.

Every person on this world is carrying emotional baggage. A key difference between pursuers and strugglers is this:

Pursuers live and act IN SPITE of their past and present issues, while strugglers live IN them.

Let me explain this important point. There are people who experience so much pain that living can be unbearable. I understand that is real; I was there. Please don't misinterpret this message as insensitive or naïve. I completely get it that some people do have lives more difficult than others. I understand that some people are faced with more to overcome, but history shows us that many of the world's most influential people realized that despite their personal difficulties, they still had the resolve and fight to choose their path—a path that impacted history.

Ignitor For Change

Your spouse threatens to leave you, your child almost dies in a careless accident, you barely escape out of a financial disaster, all of these situations can be labeled a crisis. What happens after a crisis occurs? The event triggers change. An underestimated differentiator of pursuers is they do not need a crisis to drive change.

Pursuers are constantly seeking out change in an effort to improve.

Strugglers need a crisis for change because they have not chosen to motivate themselves. It's happened to most of us. We feel the need to start new only after a major event pushes us to that extreme point. Initiating change without a crisis is much more difficult because it requires higher amounts of discipline. But pursuers find their motivation as the only tool necessary.

Catastrophizing

While at grandpa and grandma's house, my two-year-old niece was out playing in the backyard. Grandma pointed out the hummingbird feeder to Ally and explained that little birds called hummingbirds would come there to eat. A short time later as she was playing, she noticed a bird flying to the bird feeder. She quickly stopped, pointed and yelled, "Look! It's a hawk!" After grandma composed herself she told Ally that it was actually a hummingbird and described how they are much smaller than a hawk. This cute story serves as a dynamic illustration of how we catastrophize things to be bigger than they are.

**Any event, idea, thing, or behavior
is exactly as big as we make it to be.**

Strugglers are experts in turning minors into majors. An everyday, common mishap will easily morph into an insurmountable challenge.

On a Monday morning, I was speaking with a struggler on the phone. I asked how their weekend was. "It was okay," they muttered. "What happened? Is everything OK?" I asked, concerned thinking something quite major had gone down. "Well," they said, "the back of my chair broke, and I spent three hours fixing it on Saturday. Kind of ruined my weekend."

**You always have a choice in how you will react
after something happens to you.**

A tire blows out, a toothache needs to be worked on, or your kid needs money for a field trip. There are thousands of minor things that flood our lives everyday. Isn't it fair to assume that these types of things happen to everyone? Who is immune to a blow out? Do "successful" people inherit teeth with no cavities?

Let's identify two reasons why strugglers so easily turn minor mishaps into catastrophes:

1. Since strugglers typically do not plan effectively, they are living in survival mode. Living paycheck to paycheck does not leave room for "accidents." When something comes up, it turns into a major event because they are unprepared.

2. Instead of devising a plan on how to attack a minor inconvenience, strugglers stew in it and can't believe it happened to them. They hem and haw and mentally shut down. Pursuers on the other hand, look at the problem and figure out how they can address it quickly so they can move on.

No one is exempt from life's inconveniences. How will you choose to deal with them? It is only major if you make it major!

Understanding Currency of Rewards

Have you ever noticed that the fulfillment in a reward is equal to the difficulty of the journey? What are some of the most difficult obstacles you have overcome? When you did, wasn't the fulfillment equal to the effort?

The greater the accomplishment, the more fulfillment we have.

Pursuers understand this concept. That is why we are more likely to see a pursuer willing to push through the hard slogging. Pursuers get it that in order to receive their "success," they are going to have to overcome the necessary adversity that will give them the equivalent reward. It can not be considered a coincidence then that pursuers are more likely to create success. It is because they are more willing to put in the effort required to satisfy the necessary work required. A life of pleasure, healthy relationships, or success at work will only bring the fulfillment if you are willing to put in the effort on the other side. I have seen too many strugglers who know what they want but just do not understand they will get out exactly what they put in.

If you want great results in anything, you must be willing to sacrifice what it takes to get that reward.

Attaining big is never easy. Attainment is only easy when the reward is small. But most often life offers us a fair trade; a hard journey equals big rewards, while the easy road equals small rewards.

Anti-Inertia Challenge

Pick an area of your life where you are a struggler. What is your plan to become a pursuer in this area?

What do your actions reveal about what is going on inside?

What do you want? What is the price? Are you willing to pay it?

Are you attracting what you want to attract?

This week, record a minor distraction that you kept minor.

How are you planning for your future?

CHANGE YOUR CHOICES
CHANGE YOUR LIFE

Understand the power in choice. Realize you can harness
that power to create your life.

Our lives are a predictable result of a cycle we
unknowingly exercise constantly.

There is a "why" behind every choice we make.

Truly understanding ourselves is an essential aspect of
choice making.

Choices are governed by universal laws. We need to be
aware how they work and grasp their impact.

Specific behaviors differentiate people who live in fulfillment
versus those who don't.

**We all deal with adversity. How we choose to
deal with it is the critical factor.**

Choosing to exercise courage, discipline, a positive attitude,
and persistence are vital to our choice-making foundation.

Choice making becomes clear after we identify our desired
outcome and detail specific steps to get there.

Chapter Seven

STORMY WEATHER

You have the power to choose your response to anything that happens to you. It's not what happens to you, it's your chosen response.

The Blind Man's Cane

"The sun was shining in my eyes, and I could barely see to do the necessary task that was allotted me. Resenting the vivid glow, I started to complain. When all at once upon the air, I heard the blind man's cane."
Earl Mussleman

I went to the gym fighting negative feelings all day. For whatever reason, I was a bit down and was having a hard time getting myself out of "it." It was one of those days where we think we have it really bad, but we really don't. You've had those days right? As I was running on the treadmill, I could see a man out of the corner of my eye walking very slowly and deliberately, literally sluffing along on the treadmill. As I turned my full attention to him, I saw a pair of walking crutches leaned against his machine. This man exercising had a severe disability in his lower body which hindered his ability to pick up his feet while he walked. I couldn't decide if I should be thankful for what I had or be fuming at myself for being worried about my "mood," which was so irrelevant. It reminded me, no one has an easy road. We all have hard issues to deal with, but this man really had a difficult road. However, his action, determination, and will were very inspiring to me.

When we decide we are going to pursue a new road, our initial excitement propels us through any minor bumps. Making a choice to change does not mean the road will be easy. In fact, choosing to do something is the easiest part. All roads consist of adversity and require a strong commitment to rededicate ourselves everyday.

**The day I decided I was finished being a victim
it only gave me direction for my behavior;
the actual decision itself did not make any changes.**

The choice to move forward in a different light serves only as the foundation for which to proceed. Similar to building a house, we must have that foundation, for upon it all other parts rest. The choice is important initially, but then has no credence shortly thereafter. The choice doesn't produce any results. It works as a catapult. The choice holds significance in the way that it provides our underlying purpose by which future decisions can be based upon. But after that, it is all up to action. I thought of this crippled man, who everyday must fight so many mental blocks just to get out of his house. He has obviously made a choice to make the best of what he has, but that is only the beginning, the foundation. Everyday, he must choose again if and how he will deal with his disability. He has to continually rededicate himself to what he wishes to accomplish.

Adversity's severity comes in wide variances, but nonetheless, we all experience it. Some challenges we bring on by choices we make, while other problems are a result of nothing but fate. Life does not come with any guarantee of smooth sailing. But we can all agree that:

Life will have challenges, and we must learn to deal with them!

A chapter is dedicated to adversity for two reasons:

1. Many adversities are unavoidable and, therefore, we are all subject to it.

2. Our choice in how we react to it is critical.

Adversity's Brilliance

A friend and I were swapping divorce horror stories. For him, he was healed and had moved on. Mine was fresh, so there was still raw and unsettled emotion. Sensing my unresolved anger, he began to explain that every adversity he has experienced in his life has turned out later to help him in some capacity. He then explained to me:

Life will teach you all the lessons you need to learn when you are open to learning them.

I acted like I knew what he was talking about when he said it, even though I didn't have a clue, nor did I really care. But later on as I reflected on the countless lessons I learned, that statement has come to be true. There were so many things I needed to learn that I never would have been able to had it not been for experiencing adversity's worst.

Being overly critical of myself and others, truly empathizing in others' pain, having a more realistic picture of life, character building, becoming more flexible to the twists and turns of life are just some of the lessons I was taught by this invaluable experience. For some time I couldn't get myself to think about learning from such pain, but after I made the decision to learn as much as I could, powerful lessons quickly became clear. It taught me that as long as I am open to learning, there will always be lessons to learn.

Try this for one day. When you wake up tell yourself, "Today I am going to learn as much as I can." When I take that approach I find it amazing how my perspective and attitude change. I become more inquisitive and watchful to my surroundings. My brain actually looks for things I could learn. Life will teach you what you need to learn. Open yourself up to its lessons so you don't miss school!

Either You Use Adversity or It Uses You

I began my career in outside sales the day after I graduated from college. Figuring now that I had a very expensive piece of paper, I had to justify it somehow and do something with my life. I didn't really know what to do, so when I was offered a job in sales "why not" was my answer. Besides, how could I turn down a starting salary of $24,000!

Twenty-one years old, zero accounts, no sales training, no sales manager. Wasn't a recipe I would say filled me with visions of success, but I was determined to figure the sales game out. If others could do it, I knew I could as well. A vital piece I picked up quickly was in order to be successful I would need to dissect every "no" and figure out what to do differently the next time to turn it into a "yes." I knew some "no's" could not be overcome, but others could, and those were the "no's" I wanted to win. It didn't happen overnight, but I soon began to change how I perceived "no's." I decided to look at every "no" as its own lesson. What could I learn from it? What could I do different next time to achieve a different result? What happened this time? Opening myself up to learning what the negative experiences really were allowed me to sharpen my process much quicker than if I only had paid attention to the times I succeeded. We can improve how we do anything by paying close attention to our failures. The failures contain the best information! So what's the secret?

Use adversity to your advantage.

See, adversity in any capacity, can either drive us down or we can learn from it. Picture the lessons of adversity like a wet mop. This mop is different, though, because the water it soaks up is valuable water. It is the water of life! You get to ring it out and get as much water out as possible. But if we just let the mop sit there, the water will never come out of the mop. The water was there for us to take, but we didn't take what was right in front of us! It is our choice and there for the taking. Adversity plays no favorites. Adversity did temporarily succeed at driving me into the ground, but once I was able to, I took back all that was mine. Figuring out how to turn adversity into an advantage can drastically reduce our learning curve and can accelerate our successes.

(If you are in sales and have trouble hearing the word "no," I strongly encourage you to read "Go For No!" by Richard Fenton.)

Two Brothers

Twin brothers grow up with a violent, abusive father. Years later, while still living in the same town they coincidentally run into a family friend who was now a professional therapist. One brother visited the old friend seeking professional help. In their initial meeting, the therapist hears the calamitous story of his life. Tragedy after tragedy finally culminated into unemployment, with nothing but the clothes on his back to show for his efforts. Prying further, the therapist asked, "How do you think you ended up here?" The brother responded, "You would too, if you were my father's son."

The therapist was expecting a lot of the same when she recognized the other twin brother a few weeks later at a convenient store. They were catching up on small talk, and she could sense this brother told a totally different story. The conversation naturally flowed to the point where the therapist was so intrigued she had to ask the same question she asked the other brother, "How do you think you ended up here?" The brother replied, "You would too, if you were my father's son."

The two brothers, having grown up in the same household, had a completely different response to their father's behavior, but the exact same response to the therapist's question. They led completely different lives as a result of their choices. The brother enjoying the more appealing life had realized at some point:

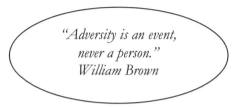

*"Adversity is an event,
never a person."*
William Brown

Tips On Dealing

Adversity comes in all shapes and sizes. But pain is pain, and regardless of how severe our story is, experience is always relative to the individual facing it. One point helping us deal with adversity is there are consistent ways of coping with it despite the individuality in experiencing it. Meaning, we all experience different scenarios in conjuction with our unique past and filters, but there are specific, universal steps we can take to help us through those trying times. Here is what helped me walk through my valley of darkness:

Think back to past difficulties and how you pushed through.

When we are dealing with a new situation, the freshness and uniqueness of it can squelch our positive thought of thinking we will get through it. It can't kill you! You have been through difficult times and made it before, and you will make it again. Look into your past. Find those victories and know you will experience that victory again.

Understand life is like a series of mountains and valleys.
When you are high on the mountaintop there might be a valley ahead,
and when you are crawling in the valley below,
you are slowly walking up a mountain to the top.

We feel untouchable when everything goes our way. Then POW! We are knocked off our feet. By the time we shake ourselves off we realize we have rolled down the entire side of a mountain and we are in the valley where it is miserably hot, dark, and uncomfortable. You might have some walking to do down in the valley, but at some point you will begin to walk up the hill toward the top again.

Someone, somewhere has been through what you are experiencing.

I hate it when I am fighting a gnarly cold and someone says, "Oh, yeah, I just had that." I think "You don't feel as crummy as I do." Adversity is unique to us because everyone has different realities that collide with their problems. There's comfort that someone else has overcome the same obstacles we are faced with. You are not alone. Someone has been where you are. Find them. They want to help you.

Find something to be thankful for – even if it is small.

There were times I couldn't find anything to be thankful for. I tried, but just couldn't. There were a couple mornings I hoped my eyes wouldn't open. I knew there were things to be thankful for, but it was just so straining to feel any gratitude. Do your best to find any little gift you see as a blessing in your life. They're out there – just look!

Acknowledge small progresses.

Twenty-four hours a day my mind was consumed in anger, wondering how my former wife could be sleeping with another man while I was sitting home in total despair. Used to having control of my life, it was scary being unable to focus my attention anywhere but my torn insides. But then, out of nowhere came breakthrough. While watching ESPN, I was able to change my focus for the first time. It was only for an instant, but it was progress! I remember being so excited that my thoughts had actually drifted away. It gave me hope that I was recovering. I knew that second would turn into minutes, and minutes into hours and then days. Look at the small ways you are dealing with your adversity and recovering. There are signs.

Don't hurry the process.

At the end of the day, any shortcut you try to take becomes a longcut. When we are walking through a difficult time we think, "I can't wait until this is over," and in an effort to avoid more pain we pretend it doesn't exist. We all want to move on with a better life. A better life though, requires us to take the time to learn the appropriate lessons. I was able to understand three valuable points as a result of walking through the eye of my storm.

1. I absorbed every possible lesson I could. I became a sponge for learning.

2. As I healed, I realized I was truly healing for the rest of my life. I was not putting on temporary band-aids that would soon fall off.

3. Like the weed that still has the root in the ground, we might as well pull out the root while we have the chance. It will be much more painful if you have to go through it again later. If we rush, we might only grab what is at the top and have to deal with collateral damage down the road.

I know "going through" it is painful, but go through the process. When it is over, you will be glad you did.

Unfortunate Coincidence

Undertaking a sales career not knowing my head from my toe and stumbling my way through a collapsed marriage were definitely the two most trying times in my life. Far from coincidence, they are also the two situations where I have learned the most valuable lessons. Coincidence? Absolutely not! I wish it wasn't the case, but the truth about adversity is:

The harder the trial, the more we learn.

Henry Beecher agrees. He said,

"One's best success comes after his greatest disappointment."

Don't get me wrong. Just because I have learned the most from those two difficult times, doesn't mean I go looking for adversity. However, my proof is in the pudding! I am married now to an amazing woman, and we enjoy a relationship I never could have imagined. Knowing this helps me take adversity with a more glancing blow each time it hits me in the face. Most importantly, I know that I CAN CHOOSE to learn from any adversity, regardless of its size, which enables me with the ability and where-with-all to negate its potentially devastating power.

Anti-Inertia Challenge

Write down adversities you have conquered in your past. What did you learn? Did you learn more from the harder times?

Take an inventory of your current troubles. How could you choose to look and deal with them differently?

Reach out to someone else who is in need. Give of yourself to others. Remember how it made you feel.

CHANGE YOUR CHOICES
CHANGE YOUR LIFE

Understand the power in choice. Realize you can harness that power to create your life.

Our lives are a predictable result of a cycle we unknowingly exercise constantly.

There is a "why" behind every choice we make.

Truly understanding ourselves is an essential aspect of choice making.

Choices are governed by universal laws. We need to be aware how they work and grasp their impact.

Specific behaviors differentiate people who live in fulfillment versus those who don't.

We all deal with adversity. How we choose to deal with it is the critical factor.

> **Choosing to exercise courage, discipline, a positive attitude, and persistence are vital to our choice making foundation.**

Choice making becomes clear after we identify our desired outcome and detail specific steps to get there.

Chapter Eight

LIFE'S IRREFUTABLES

Courage
Discipline
Attitude
Persistence

Think back to elementary math class. Remember the lowest common denominator? It's the number that would be divisible into every other number, a constant. The qualities discussed in this chapter are just the same. In examining people who get "it done," these are the lowest common denominators of what they have in common. We will refer to them as the "irrefutables," because by definition that means incontrovertible or impossible to refute, there is no argument against it. Here they are:

Courage – choosing to move into
Discipline – choosing to invest time/build skill
Attitude – choosing your mental edge
Persistence – choosing to continue through

This chapter will provide insight as to what each trait means and what they look like. I am convinced that these traits are the foundational cornerstone for us to achieve anything we want in this life, and with them, every impossible is suddenly possible! Also, consider as you read this chapter how relevant these traits are to successfully fortifying your reality wheel. A wheel that is constructed with courage, discipline, attitude, and persistence builds an unshakable core, which is needed as our realities continually receive rigorous testing.

Common Link

What do courage, discipline, attitude, and persistence have in common? By now, I bet you have a good guess! That's right, they are all qualities in life we can CHOOSE to adopt and utilize. One might be born with tendencies or a predisposition which gives them a propensity to acquire one of these traits easier than another, but nobody is born with one of them fully embodied into the fabric of their being. Anyone who at anytime exudes one or all of these qualities has CHOSEN to do so!

Becoming who or what we want to be is a *process*, not something we *possess*.

"They are so courageous," you hear someone say. Or, "they always have such a great attitude." Or, "how are they so disciplined all the time." Or, "they just never stop at no." These are all phrases we hear or think about others, and due to defensiveness or envy, we convince ourselves that is "just the way they are." Bologna. No one is just courageous, disciplined, positive, or persistent. We just don't want to admit we have the same ability to do the same.

Every time one exercises courage, discipline, a positive attitude, or persistence they choose to do so.

Some people do have hard wiring which would predispose them to adopt a trait easier than somebody else. A positive attitude for example, is a trait that can be learned, but it is also a trait that one can be genetically wired toward having. Regardless, it can be learned! Consider yourself fortunate when genetics lean in your favor, and know that you will have to work harder to generate momentum in other areas that you are not as naturally strong in.

As humans we are prone to behaving in cycles. Certain times can produce massive productivity, while during other seasons, we can feel like we couldn't accomplish a thing. We might demonstrate strong courage for a season, yet lack the discipline we desire. Or, perhaps we are disciplined but lack persistence. Whatever it is, understand we might not perfectly execute on these four traits all the time.

Here's a neat tidbit about the four irrefutable traits. When you get really good at one, others follow easier. Here's an example. Let's say you work on having a positive attitude. Don't you agree that being disciplined, persistent, and courageous will be easier if you already possess a positive attitude? How about persistence? If you develop persistence, don't you agree that courage will accompany that persistence easier than working on courage by itself?

Don't put unnecessary pressure on yourself to master the four irrefutables at once. It takes time and effort, but as you begin to work at one, the others will follow.

Irrefutable Ability #1:
Courage: Choose To Move Into

"Courage is rightly considered the foremost of the virtues because upon it, all others depend." Winston Churchill

Courage IS the cornerstone of all virtues. Anything we want to do demands courage. Any process becomes more manageable to us the more courage we grab onto. Courage comes as we invest time and energy. Courage is so vital because if you never take that first step, you will never give yourself the opportunity to take a second. Without courage, nothing would ever get started. Courage gives you the power to take that first step, which is the hardest step. From there, we don't know what will happen. Well, we do one thing that will happen if that crucial first step is not taken. You will never have a chance to get what you want. By taking a step, at least you give yourself a shot at attaining your goal. Step two is only possible after step one. When fear strikes and your courage is on the line, remember:

"We will be disappointed if we fail; but we are doomed if we don't try." Beverly Sills

Courage – Turning Intentions Into Action

"I know I should....," "I just didn't have the time, but I wanted to....," or "I really was going to do it, but then...." Remember, intentions are weak. They don't get us anywhere except to daydream land. Courage is the transition between intention and action. The defining moment of courage is when you take your intentions and act.

Making your intentions real is simply acting upon them. The difference between what you intend or want to do and doing it? COURAGE.

Courage – Eating The Frog

Imagine you had to eat a frog. You stare at its slimy skin and shiver in anticipation. The longer you look at the frog, the worse the imagined taste becomes. Your fear of eating the frog keeps getting worse the longer you stare at it.

What are the frogs in your life? What frog have you been staring at for so long that you are no longer able to eat it? The longer you stare at it without taking a bite, the worse and worse it is going to look and taste!. What is courage going to give you here? Action. What will action do? It will restore your confidence and give you momentum to move forward. I can guarantee you this: the second bite will be much easier than the first.

**As you confront your fear, it will lose its power.
The more you back away from your fear,
the more powerful it becomes.**

If I exercise consistently, it feels great. Exercise gives me energy I need and physiologically helps increase my energy levels. After three or four days of not working out, I begin to feel lethargic. I feel a huge difference in my body and mind between when I am consistently exercising and when I am not. By the fourth day of not exercising, what will make me feel better is the thing that sounds the hardest to do! Exercise! The longer I don't exercise, the more lethargic I feel. The more lethargic I feel, the less I want to exercise! Courage works the same way. The longer we remain inactive on something, the more fear we will accumulate.

The longer we wait, the more courage we will need.

"Action is a great restorer of confidence. Inaction is not only the result, but the cause of fear. Perhaps the action you take will be successful; perhaps different action or adjustments will have to follow. But any action is better than no action at all."
Norman Peale

Ask a salesperson what the quickest slump buster is and they will tell you getting a new customer. It's motivating, invigorating! But when a salesperson is in a slump, can you guess what gets harder and harder to do? Cold call! It almost feels impossible to cold call to get that new customer you need to break your slump. The deeper the slump, the more difficult the idea of finding a new customer becomes. When the time comes:

If you have to eat a frog, don't stare at it too long.

Courage – Who Said Fear Is Bad?

Fear carries with it a negative connotation, don't you think? Why is that? I think it is because most of us are not courageous in overcoming our fears. If we overcame fear 100% of the time, then fear really wouldn't be a bad thing would it? No, it is only because fear inhibits us from taking necessary action that we associate negativity with it.

Avoid feeling ashamed, guilty, regretful, or down because you have fears. Everybody feels fearful about something. Think about the last time you felt fear. What did you do? What did you say to yourself? Don't back away because you feel fear. And, just because you feel fear doesn't mean you have to back off. In fact in this case, the opposite really holds true. The more fear we feel, the more we need to act. When we feel numb by our fear, we need to act anyway. Sean Penn said:

"Whatever you fear the most is what you need to do."

Act in spite of your fear!

Once you act and take that first step, you know what happens because you have experienced it before – your fear dissipates. No matter how big your fear, being courageous still comes down to a choice. Choose to be courageous!

> *"The two things I did learn were that you are as powerful and strong as you allow yourself to be, and that the most difficult part of any endeavor is taking the first step, making the first decision."*
> *Robyn Davidson*

Irrefutable Ability #2:
Discipline: Choose to Invest Time/Build Skill

By definition the ability to be disciplined is rather simple; unfortunately, living it is not quite as easy. There aren't many secrets or profound concepts lying beneath the surface. Being disciplined is basically just doing it. If we are to more formally define discipline we could describe it as training that perfects or corrects our mental abilities, character, or behavior. Moreover, that as we buy into a prescribed pattern of behavior we gain more control or order.

Discipline – Sacrifice

Executing discipline requires that we habitually do something in order to gain something else. Since discipline requires us DOING, that means we have to NOT DO something else. Not doing something else then requires sacrifice.

A new discipline is often initiated from a new idea, belief, or want. The time it takes to be disciplined in your new task will have to be at the expense of time you used to spend doing something else. At first it will likely be easy to replace your time focusing on your new habit. But obstacles will come, and going back to old habits or an easier path will look better. That is why it is important to:

Take pride in making sacrifices

Many times, we look at sacrifices we have to make and feel sorry for ourselves. We are being disciplined in order to attain something we want right? Take pride in the fact that you are willing to make sacrifices based on your eventual prize. Imagine hitting your goal. Put yourself there; it will erase the immediate pain you are feeling and remind you why you are experiencing the discomfort.

Let's look at an example. You want to attend more of your kid's athletic events. Your boss gives you the go ahead that you can leave work an hour early on those days as long as you come in an hour early in the morning. The problem? You LOVE to sleep! Now, you have to wake up an hour earlier. You will need to be disciplined in the morning to enjoy the reward later. That's how discipline works!

The next day, your child has a game. Your alarm goes off and you think, "Ugh. I am so tired. I have to get up an hour earlier. I forgot." Don't forget why you are doing it! You are making a sacrifice to obtain a specific reward, supporting and loving your child.

You must be willing to sacrifice old, cozy, comfortable, easier things in order to get whatever it is you desire. If you aren't willing to do that, you might want to curb your expectations. Otherwise, you might be disappointed with the results. Life doesn't give us great for free!

Discipline now will bring rewards later.

Let's take discipline and apply it to something we learned about pursuers. Pursuers take the time and energy to plan for their future. What if you took thirty minutes at the beginning of every week to review the past week and plan for the upcoming week? I know you are all busy and have hundreds of commitments, but we're talking about your life here. Planning is worth the sacrifice!

During that half hour, you would be able to accomplish many things. You would see clearly where you are at. From there, you could estimate future consequences and, as a result, make necessary changes. Basically, you would discipline yourself to see your future, which provides you with the ability to make choices. From there, you can either leave things as they are or choose differently.

Discipline – Constructive Discomfort

We understand that the need to sacrifice will accompany discipline. We also know that when we give other things up in order to be disciplined, there will be some pain or discomfort associated with that because whatever we are giving up we likely enjoyed. Doing away with our comforts will cause some pain.

You decide you want to give up drinking coffee (I hope I never try that). You wake up the next morning, and the time comes when you ritualistically had your morning Joe (which, of course, sounds better than it ever has because you know you shouldn't have it). At that point, you have a choice. You can either have your cup of coffee and compromise your agenda, or go grab a cup of juice. It's only the first day, you feel guilty giving in that early, so you begrudgingly cry at the fridge and pour your juice. *The pain you feel while you drink that juice is constructive discomfort.* It's that point in time where you feel discomfort because of a sacrifice you are making. But, don't forget that it is constructive as well. As mad or disappointed as you are, remind yourself why you are making the sacrifice. It will help negate your discomfort. You are sacrificing for a later payoff, a future reward

---

When you decide to make sacrifices, anticipate and understand you will feel discomfort.

Discipline – The Battle
Comfortable Inaction vs. Productive Discomfort

This is a doozy of a fight. As you just read, when we apply ourselves to new disciplines, it is common for us to feel uncomfortable. The discomfort could come from doing something new which we are not familiar with or it could come from what we are sacrificing.

On the other side of the coin, the idea we are fighting with is the notion of comfortable inaction. It is safe to be comfortable. Not doing anything is easy. We know safe. We know comfortable. Why do I want to put myself in discomfort anyways?

You will be faced with this battle each and every time you pursue a new end. The idea of moving back to your comfort zone and not acting will look very appealing at times.

Especially the more discomfort you feel and the more sacrifices you are making. Life does not give out great rewards without us having to earn them. What that means is this:

The more discomfort you feel, the bigger your change, and the greater the reward.

In order for me to sustain a new commitment, I must rededicate myself everyday to my new cause or else it becomes too easy to throw in the towel. Don't feel guilty when you feel like giving up. You're human! That's exactly what discipline is. It's moving forward when you don't feel like doing it. That is precisely where the sacrifice comes in.

Discipline – How Do You "Feel"

Do you think Michael Jordan only took extra shots when he felt like it? Do you think Lance Armstrong only trained when he wanted to ride a bike fifty miles? Do you think anyone great in their field only worked at it when they wanted to?

The ability to be disciplined comes into play when we don't feel like doing it. If I feel like waking up at five in the morning, that isn't really discipline, because I feel like doing it. I am exercising discipline when I do NOT feel like waking up that early; then, I must exercise discipline in order to get up.

Here's the single most important factor separating successful people I have studied. They have the ability to consistently do the things they need to do regardless of how they feel.

Successful people are able to do those things which they don't feel like doing, but know they need to do.

It's really easy for me to go the gym on the weekend. But try getting me up Monday morning to go running. People who get what they want are masters at doing what they need to do, regardless of how they feel. By overcoming their feelings with discipline, they develop the consistent actions necessary to acquire their goals.

Irrefutable #3: Attitude: Choose Your Mental Edge

"You are what you think about all day long."
Emerson

The other morning as I was driving to work, I concluded that the red light gods were smiling down at me as I hit every red light. As I started to dwell on it, I became more and more frustrated every red light I came to. Something very interesting happened shortly after my latest red light temper tantrum. The next light I went through was green, but I didn't even notice it until later. Why? I was so focused on hitting all the red lights that I didn't even realize it when I went through a green.

There is significant relevance to this silly example. It may have felt like I was hitting every light red, but was I really? How many lights were green that I didn't think about? What was also remarkable was the way in which I viewed the traffic lights in their affect on my attitude. It was putting me in a bad mood. It reminded me of a powerful reality:

Our attitudes can be shaped by what we see, and by how we choose to look at them.

Attitude – Determinism

In the world of psychology there is a term called determinism. Determinism is the belief that we don't choose what happens to us, rather, we respond automatically, based on our genes, environment, and past consequences.

I don't deny that the above factors can and do influence our responses, but they don't account for all of our responses. We still have the ultimate freedom in this life. That is the ability to choose our response to any situation. Our attitude is ours to own. I am not implying that we won't have bad days or sometimes feel down. I am saying we always have a choice in our attitude. Our response to a certain situation is our chosen response to it. It is not automatic, although it may feel that way.

Attitude – Back To Beliefs

"One comes to believe whatever one repeats to oneself sufficiently often, whether the statement be true or false. It comes to be dominating thought in one's mind."
Robert Collier

Our attitudes can be so fragile. They can be blown around like a feather in a tornado. Check out your own attitude. Are you often in a bad mood? If you are, how are you are talking to yourself? My guess is you are talking to yourself not as your friend, but as a critic. When you do that, you need to go back to your personal beliefs about yourself because our life will always express our most dominant thoughts.

Our attitudes really show who we are. Our attitudes are shaped by our beliefs and thoughts. If you find yourself on the wrong side of the attitude coin more often than you'd like, revert back to your beliefs. Listen to them, analyze them, and see if you need to make some internal adjustments which will help you see the world in a better light.

Attitude – What's Inside Counts

We have all heard funny comments surrounding people who always "seem to be in a good mood." We call them cheesy, fake, or unrealistic. So, what is it about attitude that is important? Why should we even bother?

In 1970, Dr. Edward Banfield, a sociologist at Harvard, authored a book titled, "The Unheavenly City." The purpose of the study and book was for Banfield to discover how financially independent people achieved their success. Initially, Banfield was certain his research would find factors such as education, family, or genetics as the most responsible agents. But what did he find to be the most attributable factor? The attitude of the mind.

Another Harvard grad, William James, said this:

*"The greatest revolution of my generation is
the discovery that individuals, by changing
their inner attitudes of mind,
can change the outer aspects of their lives."*

Irrefutable #4: Persistence:
Choose To Continue Through

*"It is the follow through that makes the
great difference between ultimate success
and failure, because it is so easy to stop."*
Charles Kettering

Persistence – It's Right There

*It was Adam's first day in sales. We headed to a heavy retail district
where I knew he would get a quick "street education in sales." Things
got tough when we hit four consecutive "not interested's." I could sense
this was testing his fortitude, but we kept plugging. The next stop –
"Nope." "Keep walking," I encouraged him. "You never know."
Sure enough, the next stop, "Yes!"*

Your success, answer, or breakthrough
could be right around the corner.

That's the difficulty with persistence. We never know how hard or long we have to go. One can never predict with any certainty where that corner is that, when we turn it, gives our answer. Success might be around the next corner. Stay in it. Keep moving forward.

Children's Books Aren't Just For Kids

Believe it or not, one of the greatest stories illustrating persistence is a book that was read to us because we couldn't read ourselves, Green Eggs and Ham. There are few stories that catch the value in persistence like this one. If you have a copy around your place pick it up and take five minutes to read it. Or, next time you are in a bookstore go read it. The persistence demonstrated by Sam is truly admirable. So admirable, that if only we were to operate in that same spirit we. too, would never stop until our goal was reached.

When things go wrong as they sometimes will,
When the road you're trudging seems all uphill,
When the funds are low and the debts are high,
And you want to smile but you have to sigh.
When care is pressing you down a bit,
Rest if you must, but don't you quit.

Life is queer with its twists and turns,
As everyone of us sometimes learns.
And many a fellow turns about,
When he might have won had he stuck it out.
Don't give up though the pace seems slow,
You may succeed with another blow.

Often the goal is nearer than
It seems to a faint and faltering man.
Often the struggler has given up,
When he might have captured the victor's cup.
And he learned too late when the night came down,
How close he was to the golden crown.

Success is failure turned inside out,
The silver tint of the clouds of doubt.
And you never can tell how close you are,
It may be near when it seems afar.
So stick to the fight when you're hardest hit,
It's when things seem worst that you mustn't quit.

- Author unknown

Anti-Inertia Challenge

Name one thing you will "take the first step" with this week.

What do you fear the most that you feel pressed to do? What will give you the courage to do that?

What are you going to choose to be more disciplined in? What will you have to sacrifice in order to do that?

What will be your rewards of being disciplined in this area?

Identify something you have a bad attitude toward that affects your behavior. Commit to changing it for a week and see what happens.

Have you given up on something you were passionate or cared about? Challenge yourself to persist through this week.

CHANGE YOUR CHOICES
CHANGE YOUR LIFE

Understand the power in choice. Realize you can harness
that power to create your life.

Our lives are a predictable result of a cycle we
unknowingly exercise constantly.

There is a "why" behind every choice we make.

Truly understanding ourselves is an essential
aspect of choice making.

Choices are governed by universal laws. We need to be
aware how they work and grasp their impact.

Specific behaviors differentiate people who live in fulfillment
versus those who don't.

We all deal with adversity. How we choose to deal
with it is the critical factor.

Choosing to exercise courage, discipline, a positive attitude,
and persistence are vital to our choice making foundation.

> **Choice making becomes clear after we
> identify our desired outcome and detail
> specific steps to get there.**

Chapter Nine

YOUR ROAD MAP

When we identify our purpose, view, and outcome before we act, our road suddenly becomes clear. The direction provides clear criteria for making decisions which will help us achieve our goals.

The Culmination

Congratulations! You have made it to the final chapter. I hope by this point you understand more about the nature of choices, how we make them, and why we make them. You should also sense a deeper understanding of yourself, how that affects the choices you make and traits that will significantly guide your progress forward. It's now time to take all of the information we have learned and create an action plan from it. What you do with this chapter is a choice! You DO have the time. You DO have the energy. You DO have the resources. You DO have the ability. Be courageous. What do you have to lose? I believe in you and believe you can undoubtedly achieve what you desire.

Why This Chapter Is Important

Do you know the main reasons why most people don't get what they want? The first reason is because they don't specifically know what they want. Second, because they don't make a plan on how to arrive at their destination.

"Ours is a world where people don't know what they want and are willing to go through hell to get it." Don Marquis

Once you define what it is you want, the second part, creating a plan, becomes much easier. We could make plans until I jump over Pluto, but if we don't know where we want to go, those plans will be a huge waste of time.

"A clear vision, backed by definite plans, gives you a tremendous feeling of confidence and personal power." Brian Tracy

Do you recall the odds of becoming financially independent? Nineteen to one. That tells me achieving that type of success is difficult. And although many people desire that, few take the time to plan how to get there and fewer take the action to make it happen. That tells me it won't be easy. We have to get busy preparing to achieve the results and success we want.

Chapter Outline

This chapter is divided into three sections.

Section 1: You will see the foundation for your plan. This foundation consists mainly of our current reality or view and your specific, desired outcomes.

Section 2: We will discuss purpose—what it means, why it is important, and how we can create our own.

Section 3: Goals built around your purpose will be discussed. We will look at how to set them and what to set them around.

"You do not have to be great to start, but you have to start to be great."
Joe Sabah

Section I: Laying the Foundation

Moving through life without producing a personal purpose or establishing specific goals is an easy oversight but a costly mistake. Only three percent of people actually set goals (pursuers), and we presume those people are enjoying a life we would all enjoy.

Think of our need for direction similar to an airplane pilot navigating their way from one point to another. Back before the technology of today, pilots had to rely on their own vision, maps they carried, and intuition in order to know where they were. Of course, this way of flying was the only method available, but it certainly was unreliable at best. Think about what happened if it was cloudy. Thankfully for technology though, navigational aids were created to provide clarity for the pilot, *giving them a fix on where they were and the final destination.*

Without two points to connect, the pilot would be lost. The pilot must have both the beginning and end in mind in order to generate a path connecting the two together. Having the destination by itself without knowing the starting place, or only knowing where they are starting without a finish, doesn't help the pilot much. Only once both points are clear, the beginning and end, can the pilot fly with confidence.

For you, getting started with your foundation requires that we also get a "fix" on two points. They will be called your "current reality" or "view" and "outcomes."

Point 1: Your Current Reality or View

Our current reality is the home base for where we are starting from today. It's possible your situation today isn't what you expected or want, but don't justify or compromise your values; just be honest with today.

"You must begin wherever you are."
Jack Boland

The Buddhists have something they refer to as the "Right View." Part of the Right View means to see things as they really are. That means taking an honest inventory. As hard as that may be, it is vital to start where we are. If your current reality is compromised by fear or shame, your directional path to your outcomes will be different and off course.

I understand for some of us taking a close look at our current reality might bring up deep-seeded, buried emotions. Keep in mind why we are doing this exercise. You are investing in yourself, your future. When attempting this exercise most people feel one of two ways. They either say, "I don't want to see how bad my life really is and I don't want to improve it." Or, I hear, "I always felt I was the victim. Now I can see that I can control my reality and outcome." It's up to you. I hope you choose the latter.

An additional reason to take a look at our current reality is we might uncover distorted or wrong assumptions we carry. If we never stand away from and look at our paradigms, we will fail to see where we need correction. The buried treasures are well worth the digging.

Point 2: Your Outcome

As illustrated with the airline pilot, our outcome is our final destination, or a result. I love the flexibility we have in outcomes, as we can always change them. They aren't permanent. You can have outcomes that you will strive for but never accomplish, or you can have outcomes that you can achieve in only minutes. There is nothing minimizing or defining what an outcome has to be. It is up to you.

The most important aspect of an outcome is only that we define it. When we envision an outcome, we create a clear definition of where we are going from our current position. We also gain a clear criterion for making decisions. Knowing your outcome will give you clarity on what is or what is not important (Your outcomes will be created when you write out your goals coming up shortly).

Creative Tension

As we assess and identify our current reality and produce desired outcomes, we will begin to feel a sensation Peter Senge refers to as creative tension. Creative tension can be described as the feeling we have which is generated by where we are today versus where we want to be. An easy way to imagine creative tension is to think about a rubber band. One side of the band is our current reality, and the other side is what we want, or vision. As you stretch the rubber band out, taking the vision further away from reality, the tension increases. This is precisely how our reality and outcomes work. As you release the rubber band, the two ends come closer together and the tension is released. The farther apart our reality is from our outcome, the more pressure we feel. At both extremes, either having too much tension or not enough is unhealthy. Ideally, we want to be right in the middle, where a healthy, positive creative tension is developed and maintained.

Creative tension is a very good measure of where you are versus where you want to be. A healthy bit of tension seems to be just right; enough to keep stretching you to achieve more, while also maintaining a close enough proximity to your outcomes. If there is no tension, then maybe you need to set new outcomes to stretch yourself. Initiating new goals will put some healthy creative tension back in your rubber band.

Section II: Purpose

The word purpose is synonymous with mission statement, vision, or purpose statement. What we call it isn't important. What is important is what we are looking to do with it. We need to identify the values, beliefs, and ideas that will serve as a platform for our life.

Creating a purpose is important for many reasons, but there are three reasons that deserve special mentioning. First, we know that doing things we don't like to do is hard, and that requires discipline. But once we establish a purpose, our passion to fulfill that purpose hopefully transcends times when we don't feel like following through. Defining a purpose will give you clarity, and that clarity will provide you with power—power we will need when life poses challenges. When those difficult times arise, we think, "How can I do this?" A strong purpose gives you the bigger "why" and makes the "how" easier.

When we claim a purpose, our discomfort becomes subordinate to its strength.

Secondly, establishing a purpose helps you overcome fearful monsters in our path. As you progress toward a purpose, you will encounter obstacles, but your purpose contains more power than the fear.

> *"Vision is greater than baggage. Greater than the negative baggage of the past and even the accumulated baggage of the present. Tapping into this sense of vision gives you the power and the purpose to rise above the baggage and act based on what really matters most." Stephen Covey*

Direction enhances freedom. That is the third reason why purpose is important. It is paradoxical, but true. In other words, creating guidelines or constraints for ourselves will actually allow us to feel more freedom than if we were to live without any direction or purpose. I know it sounds funny, but I feel free when I have a detailed schedule outlining my activities. There is freedom in that purpose. But when I operate ambiguously, without direction, I actually feel more restricted, lost, and less free.

Claiming Your Purpose

After a devastating accident involving a drunk driver who killed her daughter, Candy Lightner took her anger and turned it into a lifelong purpose: Mothers Against Drunk Driving. Just an ordinary person with a burning desire and a powerful mission helped make MADD a very popular and effective group.

Steve Jobs, when starting up Apple didn't have a purpose of becoming rich. His mission was to create a "user-friendly" computer that would change the world. Sure, riches followed that, but in both cases success followed a mission statement that provided purpose beyond an individual. A distinction running through most effective purposes is the desire to help others. Once you can effectively do that, you will gain many other benefits associated with that success.

Here is the purpose I live by:

To help as many people as I can realize and maximize their unique potential so they may enjoy the life they deserve.

Since I tangibly created this purpose over two years ago, it truly has cleared my direction, thinking, and planning. Developing this statement has made decisions easier for me. It has given me purpose deeper than myself, and it has provided me with the fuel to move past my fears and into the world of accomplishing my dreams. Purpose propels!

Writing Your Purpose

Ideas are listed to keep them clear. They appear in no particular order.

Your purpose should include or be:

- A lifelong pursuit.
- Expressions that reflect your unique abilities, gifts, and talents.
- Able to connect to and be an extension of your goals.
- A communication of what you stand for.
- A collection of your key values.
- An answer to the question, "What really is important to me?"

Section III: Goals

Goals can be scary because they mean change, accountability, and follow through. Goals serve as our paved road to arrive at the destination of our choosing. It connects us from our view to our desired outcome.

"The only person who likes change is a wet baby."
Roger von Oech

There is endless literature on goal setting. You could find thousands of strategies outlining how to effectively goal set, all with minor tweaks and differences. The main idea is that you get your goals written down and focused on them. We could spend seven hours analyzing goals and theories, but unless we write them down and act on them, they are useless. Let's get down to business!

How To Eat An Elephant

I decided I was going to write this book. I then had a genius thought, "How?" Thousands of these ideas were floating in my head. But as I dedicated myself to actually doing it, the task became enormously large in my mind. Basically, I had to eat an elephant.

A message by Ann McIndoo called, "Discover the Author Inside You," provided me with the fork and knife I needed to start nibbling away. The concept was genius. Break all the steps down into digestible pieces and conquer them one at a time. The greatness of Ann's system lies in its simplicity. Any large goal simply needs to be broken down into eatable pieces. Eating an elephant? Break it up into small parts. Decide to eat a certain amount each day. Before you know it, you will have taken a huge chunk!

Want to lose 50 pounds? Break it up into ten goals containing five pounds each. Focus only on those five pounds. When you accomplish that, move to the next five, etc., etc.

*"All large tasks are completed
in a series of starts."*
Neil Fiore

Where To Start

Part I: Principle of the Objective. There is a military principle called the Principle of the Objective. The only requirement of this principle is that you must decide in advance what it is you want to accomplish. By deciding in advance what you want, your goal setting process becomes much easier. Simply align your goals with what you want in order to achieve it.

Part II: Project Forward. Here's a great way to get an idea of some outcomes or goals you want. Think of yourself five years from now (you can select your own timeframe). What do you want? Where do you want to be? What do you want to have accomplished? Then, slowly work your way backwards. As you work back, think about what you will need to do in order to arrive there. Your reflections will present you with your guide and direction, and should be comprised of short and middle-ranged goals.

Part III: Determine Why. After you set your goals, review them. Make sure you can explain why you want to achieve them. Are they in line with your purpose? Will they lead you to your outcomes? Ensuring alignment is critical. The more focus your path has, the harder it will be to get thrown off track.

Here We Go!

List everything you want, to be, to do, or have. Do not limit your thinking here. Get it all down on paper. Take your time. Dream WILDLY! Don't hold anything back.

Categorize them into time segments. This could be short, medium, and long.

Check your list for balance in life. Try and avoid being too heavy in one area. For instance, if you have 15 goals and 14 of them are career based, try and even it out.

Prioritize your goals. You can't do everything at once. What is truly important to you? Which goals should you focus on first? What can't wait?

Make a daily, weekly, monthly, or yearly tracker. Write out how you will achieve your goals.

Here are some more tips as you journey toward your new outcomes:

- Cross out goals when you accomplish them and celebrate your victories. Small goals are important, too. Celebrate your successes!

- Prepare for unexpected events that may change your goals or your progress. Make the necessary modifications and move on. Your goals are not permanent, but accomplishing should be!

- Review your goals as often as you can. Get them in your mind. The more you feed yourself with that information the quicker your life, mind, and actions will move toward you achieving those ends.

Do you see how our picture completes itself? Just like eating an elephant, we took all of the pieces (view, purpose, and outcome), broke them down into small bite-size pieces, and now we have a comprehensive plan to start new.

We have one more step to add to the equation. What do we know is going to be the critical factor as we journey forward? I'll give you a hint. It's what this book is about. You will be faced with choices constantly. And, along with choices we know that the road to your outcomes might not be like going on vacation. What are you going to need and use as you travel from point one to point two? Yes, "the irrefutables." Our picture is now complete.

Let's review our steps:

Step 1: We start with an accurate view or current reality of our life as it is now.

Step 2: We create our defining purpose(s), which serve as an overriding guide to our desired outcomes.

Step 3: We set our goals that will connect our current reality to our outcomes.

Step 4: Accomplish! Act!

The Choice Is Yours!

Your hopes can become your reality. Without them being possible, we wouldn't have the ability to imagine them.

To your chosen life,

My sincere hope is that the material in this book helps empower you to harness the freedom and power you possess to choose your life. The choices we make have a profound impact on our lives, yet, we live each day not understanding choices or ourselves enough to comprehend how they affect us. It is imperative for us to take full responsibility for our choices; they make our lives. You do have the ability to control the choices you make. In turn, you will create the life you want.

In our hurried lives, we rarely stop to think about how we make choices or how they are creating our reality. As a result, we end up in places we wouldn't choose to be. Wherever you end up, there is always hope. Hope for a better future because we can choose new at anytime.

Understand the road leading to your desired destination will not be a straight, easy road. There will be difficulties as you move out of your comfort zones and into unchartered territories. Take those times of discomfort as a subtle reminder that you are experiencing growing pains. Be okay with mistakes along the way; they're inevitable and will help refine your process. Be proud of yourself as you try and better your life. We are all works in progress.

We are all trying to get better. Perfection will never be achieved, but doing our best to achieve it can be!

I Want To Hear From You!

Nothing would make me more excited than to hear real stories detailing how you used personal choice to change your life! Drop me an email explaining what happened, what you plan to do, what changed, or any other news surrounding your personal growth. I want to share in your journey and excitement alongside you.

feedback@markheerema.com

Mark Heerema

Mark Heerema is the creator and founder of Life Impact Training. L.I.T.'s mission is to help as many people possible realize and live their life fulfilling their full, unique potential. Executing on his passion to help others is a desire Mark has felt compelled to do ever since he began coaching sales professionals early in his career. Prior to that, Mark polished his selling skills while successfully climbing up the corporate ladder of a quickly growing sales-based organization.

Mark began his sales career at 21 and was soon setting company sales records, which resulted in a promotion to sales management. Continuing in his quest to better equip himself with the necessary tools to effectively coach others, Mark then completed his Master's Degree in Arts Management, while simultaneously journeying through a devastating personal loss.